EDUCATING THE ENGINEER OF 2020

ADAPTING ENGINEERING EDUCATION TO THE NEW CENTURY

NATIONAL ACADEMY OF ENGINEERING
OF THE NATIONAL ACADEMIES

THE NATIONAL ACADEMIES PRESS
Washington, DC
www.nap.edu

THE NATIONAL ACADEMIES PRESS   500 Fifth Street, N.W.   Washington, DC 20001

NOTICE: To arrive at the findings and recommendations of this report, the National Academy of Engineering has used a process that involves careful selection of a balanced and knowledgeable committee, assembly of relevant information, and peer review of the resultant report. Over time, this process has proven to produce authoritative and balanced results.

This material is based upon work supported by the National Science Foundation under Grant No. 0242173, with contributions from the Hewlett Packard Company, the General Electric Foundation, and the National Academy of Engineering Fund. Any opinions, findings and conclusions, or recommendations expressed in this material are those of the authors and do not necessarily reflect the views of the sponsoring organizations.

Library of Congress Cataloging-in-Publication Data

Educating the engineer of 2020 : adapting engineering education to the new century / National Academy of Engineering of the National Academies.
    p. cm.
    ISBN 0-309-09649-9 (pbk.) — ISBN 0-309-55006-8 (pdf) 1. Engineering—Study and teaching (Higher)—United States. I. National Academy of Engineering.
    T73.E37 2005
    620′.00711—dc22
                        2005023673

Additional copies of this report are available from the National Academies Press, 500 Fifth Street, N.W., Lockbox 285, Washington, DC 20055; (800) 624-6242 or (202) 334-3313 (in the Washington metropolitan area); Internet, http://www.nap.edu.

THE NATIONAL ACADEMIES
Advisers to the Nation on Science, Engineering, and Medicine

The **National Academy of Sciences** is a private, nonprofit, self-perpetuating society of distinguished scholars engaged in scientific and engineering research, dedicated to the furtherance of science and technology and to their use for the general welfare. Upon the authority of the charter granted to it by the Congress in 1863, the Academy has a mandate that requires it to advise the federal government on scientific and technical matters. Dr. Ralph J. Cicerone is president of the National Academy of Sciences.

The **National Academy of Engineering** was established in 1964, under the charter of the National Academy of Sciences, as a parallel organization of outstanding engineers. It is autonomous in its administration and in the selection of its members, sharing with the National Academy of Sciences the responsibility for advising the federal government. The National Academy of Engineering also sponsors engineering programs aimed at meeting national needs, encourages education and research, and recognizes the superior achievements of engineers. Dr. Wm. A. Wulf is president of the National Academy of Engineering.

The **Institute of Medicine** was established in 1970 by the National Academy of Sciences to secure the services of eminent members of appropriate professions in the examination of policy matters pertaining to the health of the public. The Institute acts under the responsibility given to the National Academy of Sciences by its congressional charter to be an adviser to the federal government and, upon its own initiative, to identify issues of medical care, research, and education. Dr. Harvey V. Fineberg is president of the Institute of Medicine.

The **National Research Council** was organized by the National Academy of Sciences in 1916 to associate the broad community of science and technology with the Academy's purposes of furthering knowledge and advising the federal government. Functioning in accordance with general policies determined by the Academy, the Council has become the principal operating agency of both the National Academy of Sciences and the National Academy of Engineering in providing services to the government, the public, and the scientific and engineering communities. The Council is administered jointly by both Academies and the Institute of Medicine. Dr. Ralph J. Cicerone and Dr. Wm. A. Wulf are chair and vice chair, respectively, of the National Research Council.

www.national-academies.org

Acknowledgments

About the National Science Foundation

The National Science Foundation (NSF) was established in 1950 by the Congress and is the only federal agency dedicated to supporting education and fundamental research in all science and engineering disciplines. The mission of NSF is to ensure that the United States maintains leadership in scientific discovery and the development of new technologies. NSF promotes the progress of engineering in the United States in order to enable the nation's capacity for innovation and to support the creation of wealth and a better quality of life.

About the Hewlett-Packard Company

Hewlett-Packard (HP) Company engages with the higher education community and leading academic institutions in many ways. From research interaction and student recruitment to customer relationships and policy advocacy, numerous HP organizations and hundreds of HP employees advance the company's interests with higher education globally.

University Relations, a unit of HP Labs, works to add value to the corporation and its partners through these various company engagements. University Relations cultivates close relationships with HP's academic partners and aligns trends in education with HP's technology and business directions. University Relations articulates company positions in higher-education forums, manages strategic technology initiatives, builds market presence with thought leaders, and facilitates high-level engagement with partner institutions.

About the General Electric Foundation

The GE Foundation, the philanthropic organization of the General Electric Company, works to strengthen educational access, equity, and quality for disadvantaged youth globally; and supports GE employee and retiree giving and involvement in GE communities around the world. In 2004, the GE Family contributed more than $150 million to community and educational programs, including $52 million from the GE Foundation. For information, visit *www.gefoundation.com*.

COMMITTEE ON THE ENGINEER OF 2020, PHASE II

G. WAYNE CLOUGH (NAE), *Chair*, Georgia Institute of Technology
ALICE M. AGOGINO (NAE), University of California, Berkeley
MARK DEAN (NAE), IBM Corporation
DEBORAH GRUBBE, BP
RANDY HINRICHS, Microsoft Corporation
SHERRA E. KERNS, Olin College
ALFRED MOYE, Hewlett-Packard Company
DIANA NATALICIO, University of Texas, El Paso
SIMON OSTRACH (NAE), Case Western Reserve University
ERNEST T. SMERDON (NAE), University of Arizona
KARAN L. WATSON, Texas A&M University
DAVID WISLER (NAE), GE Aircraft Engines

EX OFFICIO MEMBER

STEPHEN W. DIRECTOR (NAE), Drexel University

NAE PROGRAM OFFICE STAFF

RICHARD TABER, Project Officer
LANCE DAVIS (NAE), Executive Officer
NORMAN FORTENBERRY, Director, Center for the Advancement of
    Scholarship on Engineering Education
NATHAN KAHL, Project Assistant
PROCTOR REID, Director, Program Office

COMMITTEE ON ENGINEERING EDUCATION

STEPHEN W. DIRECTOR (NAE), *Chair*, Drexel University
JOHN R. BIRGE, University of Chicago
ANJAN BOSE (NAE), Washington State University
ANTHONY BRIGHT, Harvey Mudd College
BARRY C. BUCKLAND (NAE), Merck Research Laboratories
MICHAEL CORRADINI (NAE), University of Wisconsin, Madison
JENNIFER SINCLAIR CURTIS, University of Florida
JAMES W. DALLY (NAE), University of Maryland
RUTH A. DAVID (NAE), ANSER Corporation
ANN Q. GATES, University of Texas, El Paso
RANDY HINRICHS, Microsoft Corporation
JAMES H. JOHNSON, Howard University
LARRY V. McINTIRE (NAE), Georgia Institute of Technology
LINDA PETZOLD (NAE), University of California, Santa Barbara
ESTHER TAKEUCHI (NAE), Wilson Greatbatch Technologies, Inc.

EX OFFICIO MEMBERS

CRAIG R. BARRETT (NAE), Chairman, National Academy of
 Engineering
RALPH J. CICERONE (NAS), President, National Academy of
 Sciences
HARVEY V. FINEBERG (IOM), President, Institute of Medicine
SHEILA E. WIDNALL (NAE), Vice President, National Academy of
 Engineering
WM. A. WULF (NAE), President, National Academy of Engineering

REVIEW COMMITEE

This report was reviewed by individuals chosen for their diverse perspectives and technical expertise, in accordance with procedures approved by the National Academies. The purpose of this independent review is to provide candid and critical comments that will assist the authoring committee and the National Academy of Engineering in making the published report as sound as possible and to ensure that the report meets institutional standards for objectivity, evidence, and responsiveness to the charge for this activity. The contents of the review comments and draft manuscripts remain confidential to protect the integrity of the deliberative process.

ELEANOR BAUM, The Cooper Union
JAY BROCKMAN, University of Notre Dame
PAUL CITRON, Medtronic, Incorporated
CANDIS CLAIBORN, Washington State University
DELORES ETTER, United States Naval Academy
MARIO GONZALEZ, University of Texas, Austin
FRANK HUGHES, Boeing Corporation (retired)
MARSHALL JONES, General Electric Company
GRANGER MORGAN, Carnegie Mellon University
WARREN SEERING, Massachusetts Institute of Technology
THOMAS SKALAK, University of Virginia

REPORT REVIEW MONITOR

ROBERT F. SPROULL, Sun Microsystems, Incorporated

Preface

The Engineer of 2020 Project centers on an effort to envision the future two decades from now, to use this knowledge in an attempt to predict the roles engineers will play in the future, and to position engineering education in the United States for what lies ahead, rather than waiting for time to pass and then trying to respond. It is driven by concern that engineering students of today may not be appropriately educated to meet the demands that will be placed on the engineer of 2020 and that, without refocusing and reshaping the undergraduate engineering learning experience, America's engineering preeminence could be lost. It takes as a given that the nation's societal goals will not be met absent a robust engineering community in the country. It asks what restructuring of program, reallocation of resources, and refocusing of faculty and professional society time and energy are required so that our educational infrastructure can educate engineers prepared to tackle the challenges of the future. It questions how we can more effectively share with students—current and potential—our passion for designing systems, structures, and devices to solve problems and our conviction that engineering is a profession that offers rich rewards for serving the interests of society.

In addressing a Summit on Engineering Education held in conjunction with this project in July 2004, Massachusetts Institute of Technology President Charles Vest encouraged the assembled educators and stakeholders to think about the students when considering how the engineering education system should be reengineered by stating, "This is the most exciting period in human history for science and engineering. The explosive advances in knowledge, instrumentation, communication, and computational capabilities create a mind-boggling playing field for the next generation. . . . As we think about the plethora of challenges, it is important, in my view, to remember that students are driven by passion, curiosity, engagement, and dreams. . . . Despite our best efforts to plan their education, to a large extent we simply help to wind them up, and then step back to watch the amazing results." Gretchen Kalonji, professor of materials science and engineering at the University of Washington, expanded on Vest's desire to engage the passion and curiosity of students stating that "[a]s we move forward, I think we need to undertake a far more bold reformulation of engineering education. Bluntly speaking, with existing models, we are losing the battle for the imagination of our youth. . . . What I would argue for is a dramatic and fundamental transformation of the educational process."

Originated and chartered by the Committee on Engineering Education of the National Academy of Engineering (NAE), the Engineer of 2020 Project consists of two parts, the first related to the development of a vision for engineering and the work of the engineer in 2020. A report of the first phase was published in the spring of 2004. The second part, the subject of this report, is to examine engineering education, in the broadest context, and ask what it needs to do to enrich the education of engineers who will practice in 2020. This initiative is not unique in that other groups have somewhat similar efforts under way or have recently completed them. The work of NAE differs in that it considers the issues with respect to all the diverse branches of engineering and examines them from the broadest possible perspective. Its principal focus is on the future of undergraduate engineering education in this country, although it is appreciated that to understand the full perspective, engineering practice and engineering education must be considered within a global context.

A Steering Committee for the Phase II project was established in February 2004 by the NAE president to guide the work. The committee met in July 2004, coincident with the Summit on Engineering Education, which was held at the National Academies' Constitution Avenue location in Washington, D.C., attended by approximately 100 participants. As background information for the summit, a series of papers was prepared by education experts on a variety of subjects, including cooperative education, the National Science Foundation engineering education coalitions, the Olin College experience, diversity, the Greenfield Coalition, the Pedagogies of the Professions Program of the Carnegie Foundation, accreditation systems, and the history of efforts to realign engineering education. These papers are included in Appendix A.

The Summit featured keynote addresses by Ruth David, Charles Vest (see Appendix B), Shirley Ann Jackson, and Nicholas Donofrio and, between the plenary sessions of the Summit, five breakout groups met to allow more detailed and interactive discussions on various aspects of the engineering education system. The Summit agenda is in Appendix C.

Immediately following the workshop, the Steering Committee met to review the workshop discussions and was assigned the task of preparing this report. Final review of the report by the Steering Committee to critique its conclusions and recommendations was conducted by e-mail.

It is notable that the Phase I report posits a statement of aspirations for the engineer of 2020 and closes with a statement of attributes thought suitable for the engineer of 2020 that match the aspirations. These aspirations and attributes express a bold optimism for the engineering profession if it is willing to confront the possibilities for the future and to prepare for them.

Ahead lies the challenge of debating and adopting, where appropriate, the recommendations of this report for adapting engineering education to the new century. The committee recognizes that "one size does not fit all" and has attempted to suggest a suite of interventions, not all of which will work in every institution. We expect that debate on these interventions will take place over the course of the coming year and we hope that their introduction into the engineering education infrastructure will rapidly follow so that today's students will indeed be prepared to practice engineering effectively in 2020.

Contents

Executive Summary

This report is the result of an initiative of the National Academy of Engineering that attempts to prepare for the future of engineering by asking the question, "What will or should engineering education be like today, or in the near future, to prepare the next generation of students for effective engagement in the engineering profession in 2020?" It accepts as a given that, first and foremost, engineering education must produce technically excellent and innovative graduates, but it does not attempt to define a "core" curriculum, recognizing that individual institutions need to design their own. It asks, rather, how to enrich and broaden engineering education so that those technically grounded graduates will be better prepared to work in a constantly changing global economy. It notes the importance of improving the recruitment and retention of students, and making the learning experience more meaningful to them. It discusses the value of considering changes in engineering education in the broader context of enhancing the status of the engineering profession and improving the public understanding of engineering.

Although the report comments on education beyond the baccalaureate, its primary focus is undergraduate education, not the academic engineering research enterprise. The success of academic engineering research is undeniable. It helped shape this nation's industrial capabilities and it continues to do so in an increasing degree as more complex products and systems based on advanced technologies are emerging in

1

the marketplace and in the social and economic infrastructure. Many of the most hi-tech companies have been spun off from university research. The end of the Cold War and the shift from defense work has put pressure on university research to accept funding from industry for shorter term product- or process-oriented research. Meanwhile, industry has decreased its own in-house fundamental engineering research, making it even more important that universities conduct advanced basic research. Thus, this is a part of the engineering education infrastructure that must be preserved, but, at the same time, it must not lead to the neglect of the undergraduate engineering education experience. Indeed, if domestic engineering students are energized by their undergraduate education experience, it will enhance the possibility that they will be retained and graduate as engineers *and* aspire to advanced degrees through the academic engineering research enterprise.

In response to the issues facing undergraduate engineering education, the committee presents a suite of recommendations in this report, including the following:

- The B.S. degree should be considered as a preengineering or "engineer in training" degree.
- Engineering programs should be accredited at both the B.S. and M.S. levels, so that the M.S. degree can be recognized as the engineering "professional" degree.
- Institutions should take advantage of the flexibility inherent in the EC2000 accreditation criteria of ABET, Incorporated (previously known as the Accreditation Board for Engineering and Technology) in developing curricula, and students should be introduced to the "essence" of engineering early in their undergraduate careers.
- Colleges and universities should endorse research in engineering education as a valued and rewarded activity for engineering faculty and should develop new standards for faculty qualifications.
- In addition to producing engineers who have been taught the advances in core knowledge and are capable of defining and solving problems in the short term, institutions must teach students how to be lifelong learners.
- Engineering educators should introduce interdisciplinary learn-

ing in the undergraduate curriculum and explore the use of case studies of engineering successes and failures as a learning tool.

- Four-year schools should accept the responsibility of working with local community colleges to achieve workable articulation[1] with their two-year engineering programs.
- Institutions should encourage domestic students to obtain M.S. and/or Ph.D. degrees.
- The engineering education establishment should participate in efforts to improve public understanding of engineering and the technology literacy of the public and efforts to improve math, science, and engineering education at the K-12 level.
- The National Science Foundation should collect or assist collection of data on program approach and student outcomes for engineering departments/schools so that prospective freshman can better understand the "marketplace" of available engineering baccalaureate programs.

The report is grounded by the observations, questions, and conclusions presented by the Phase I report, *The Engineer of 2020: Visions of Engineering in the New Century.* That report begins with a review of the likely technological changes and challenges that will impact the world and the engineering profession. It notes that a dramatic expansion of knowledge is expected that offers exciting opportunities for engineering to develop new technologies to address the problems faced by society. It addresses the societal, geopolitical, and professional context within which engineering and its new technologies will exist. It notes that the coming era will be characterized by rapid population growth, which will contain internal dynamics that may affect world stability as well as the types of problems engineers will face. Growth will be concentrated in less developed countries where a "youth bulge" will occur, whereas in advanced countries the population will age. Issues related to improving quality of life through advanced technologies in some countries will be

---

[1]Articulation agreements establish rules that govern transfer credits that students earn at one institution (typically the community college) and are recognized and accepted by the partner institution (typically a four-year institution) for particular major courses of study.

contrasted with more basic problems such as access to water and housing in others. Within countries, the demographics will change, including in the United States, where the numbers of minorities will grow rapidly whereas those of the traditional majority will decline in a relative sense. This has major implications for the future of engineering, a profession where minorities and women remain underrepresented.

Although certain basics of engineering will not change, the explosion of knowledge, the global economy, and the way engineers will work will reflect an ongoing evolution that began to gain momentum a decade ago. The economy in which we will work will be strongly influenced by the global marketplace for engineering services, evidenced by the outsourcing of engineering jobs, a growing need for interdisciplinary and system-based approaches, demands for new paradigms of customization, and an increasingly international talent pool. The steady integration of technology in our public infrastructures and lives will call for more involvement by engineers in the setting of public policy and in participation in the civic arena. The external forces in society, the economy, and the professional environment will all challenge the stability of the engineering workforce and affect our ability to attract the most talented individuals to an engineering career. However, amid all these challenges, exciting opportunities also will exist if the engineering community takes the initiative to prepare for the future.

If the United States is to maintain its economic leadership and be able to sustain its share of high-technology jobs, it must prepare for this wave of change. Although there is no consensus at this stage, it is agreed that innovation is the key and engineering is essential to this task; but engineering will only contribute to success if it is able to continue to adapt to new trends and provide education to the next generation of students so as to arm them with the tools needed for the world as it will be, not as it is today. It is within this context that this Phase II report considers recommendations for changes in engineering education.

Reinventing engineering education requires the interaction of engineers in industry and academe. The entire engineering enterprise must be considered so that the changes made result in an effective system. Because most engineers work in industry and do not interact one-on-one with people who directly benefit from their services, as do physicians, lawyers, and teachers, the public is unclear about what most engineers do, and secondary students (and their parents and advisors) have poorly formed ideas about what an engineering education offers and how they can serve society through engineering practice. Engineering needs to develop iconic images that the public immediately recognize and respond to in a positive way. Those "icons" should include simple images of the options for engineering education, their implications for future career paths, and the image of a person who never stops learning.

This report is intended to begin a dialog about reinventing engineering education, but it makes recommendations that are broader than the curricular challenges indicated in the Phase I report. In the spirit of considering engineering education as a system and as part of a system of systems, consideration is given herein to important factors such as improving the public's understanding of engineering, its technological literacy, and K-12 education, which can have an important but indirect effect on engineering in terms of encouraging secondary school students to consider an engineering education and preparing them intellectually so that an engineering education is accessible to them.

1

Phase I Revisited

As a prelude to considering formulation of recommendations for the reengineering of engineering education, the Phase I committee imagined how the context of engineering practice may change by 2020. A brief summary of their observations is provided below.

THE PACE OF TECHNOLOGICAL CHANGE

Change is constant, but, on an absolute basis, our world has changed more in the past 100 years than in all those preceding. By the end of the twentieth century, the developed world had become a healthier, safer, and more productive place, a place where engineering, through technology, had forged an irreversible imprint on our lives and our identity.

Scientific and engineering knowledge presently doubles every 10 years (Wright, 1999). This geometric growth rate has been reflected in an accelerating rate of technology introduction and adoption. Product cycle times continue to decrease, and each cycle delivers more functional and often less expensive versions of existing products, and occasionally introducing entirely new "disruptive" technologies. Older technologies are becoming obsolete at an increasing rate. Recent and emergent advances, such as those in biotechnology, nanotechnology, information and communications technology, material science and photonics, and other totally unanticipated technologies will be among the changes with which engineering and engineering education will need to contend leading up to 2020 and beyond.

CONTINUING CHALLENGES

The engineer of 2020 will need to learn much new technical information and techniques and be conversant with and embrace a whole realm of new technologies, but some old problems are not going to go away. They will demand new attention and, perhaps, new technologies. In some cases, their continuing neglect will move them from problems to crises.

Although the United States has arguably had the best physical infrastructure in the developed world, the concern is that these infrastructures are in serious decline. Because it is of more recent vintage, the nation's information and telecommunications infrastructure has not suffered nearly as much degradation, but vulnerabilities of the infrastructure (or infrastructures) due to accidental or intentional events are well recognized and a serious concern. Natural resource and environmental concerns will continue to frame our world's challenges. For example, in 2020 the state of California will need the equivalent of 40 percent more electrical capacity, 40 percent more gasoline, and 20 percent more natural gas energy than was needed in the year 2000 (CABTH, 2001). Forty-eight countries containing a total of 2.8 billion people could face freshwater shortages by 2025 (Hinrichsen et al., 1997). The populations of developed countries will "age" and engineering can be an agent for developing assistive technologies for aging citizens to help them maintain healthy, productive lifestyles well beyond conventional retirement age.

SOCIAL CONTEXT OF ENGINEERING PRACTICE

The future is uncertain. However, one thing is clear: Engineering will not operate in a vacuum separate from society in 2020, any more than it does now. Both on a macroscale, where the world's natural resources will be stressed by population increases, and on a microscale, where engineers need to understand how to work in teams to be effective, consideration of social issues is important to engineering.

By the year 2020, the world population will approach 8 billion people, and much of that increase will be among groups that today are outside of the developed nations (CIA, 2001).[1] Of the 1.5 billion people that the world population will gain by 2020, most will be added to countries in Asia and Africa. By 2015, and for the first time in history, the majority of people, mostly poor, will reside in urban centers, mostly in countries that lack the economic, social, and physical infrastructures to support a burgeoning population.

In the United States, if current trends continue, Hispanic Americans will account for 17 percent of the U.S. population and African Americans will constitute 12.8 percent of the population by 2020. The percentage of whites will decline from the 2000 value of 75.6 percent to 63.7 percent. Looking even further into the future, by 2050, almost half of the U.S. population will be nonwhite (USCB, 2002). Thus, in 2020 and beyond, the engineering profession will need to develop solutions that will serve an increasingly diverse community and will likely need to (and should try to) draw more students from sectors of the community that traditionally have not been well represented in the engineering workforce.

As new knowledge on health and health care is created, shifts in life expectancies will lead to an increase in the number of people living well beyond established retirement ages. With increases in life expectancy, relatively fewer young workers will be available to help pay for the services that older citizens expect to have, and stresses on economic systems will occur. An aging population makes greater demands on the health care system, heightens labor force contractions, and increases political instability (CIA, 2001). The engineering profession of 2020 will have to operate in this environment, which may include "senior" engineers who are willing and able to work, and perhaps compelled to do so because of economic necessity.

In contrast to the aging trend, nations in many politically unstable parts of the world will experience a "youth bulge," a disproportionate number of 15- to 29-year-olds in the general population; globally, more than 50 percent of the world's population could be under 18 years old in 2020. Youth-bulge conditions are likely in many regions of recent social and political tension, which are exacerbated by an excess of idle youth unable to find employment. As a consequence, the world could

---

[1]Developed nations as defined by the World Bank are countries with a gross national product equal to or greater than $10,000 per person.

face continuing social and political unrest and threats from terrorism and fundamentalism, creating an increased need for military services and security measures domestically and abroad.

Among these unfolding changes, the world's economy, which has become tightly interlinked, with much of the change triggered by technology itself, will remain so, short of worldwide military or economic warfare. In such an environment, the marketplace for engineering services will be worldwide, and jobs will move freely. Information sharing allowed by the Internet, broadband communication links, and high-speed computers has the effect of tying cultures, knowledge, and economies together with possible positive as well as negative impacts on U.S.-based engineers. For many years to come, engineers in developing economies will be willing and able to do equivalent work for less than U.S. wages. The key to maintaining a robust marketplace for U.S. engineers will be how they can bring additional value to offset this difference.

PROFESSIONAL CONTEXT FOR ENGINEERS IN THE FUTURE

In the past, steady increases in knowledge have spawned new subspecialties within engineering (e.g., microelectronics, photonics, and biomechanics). However, contemporary challenges—from biomedical devices to complex manufacturing designs to large systems of networked devices—increasingly require a systems perspective. This drives a growing need to pursue collaborations with multidisciplinary teams of technical experts. Important attributes for these teams include excellence in communication (with technical and public audiences), an ability to communicate using technology, and an understanding of the complexities associated with a global market and social context. Flexibility, receptiveness to change, and mutual respect are essential as well.

The explosion in knowledge sharing, coupled with advances in technology, will provide the ability to achieve a new era in *customerization*—a buyer-centric business strategy that combines mass customization with customized marketing (Wind and Rangaswamy, 2000). This will demand the social interaction of many engineers with customers, even more so than today, belying the image of the engineer as the "techie nerd" and demanding that such engineers have well-developed people skills in addition to their ability to solve problems.

The business competitiveness, military strength, health, and standard of living of a nation are integrally connected to engineering. As technology becomes increasingly ingrained into every facet of our lives, the convergence between engineering and public policy will also increase. This new level of interrelatedness necessitates that engineering, and engineers, develop a stronger sense of how technology and public policy interact. To date, engagement of engineers in public policy issues has been limited at best. It is both the responsibility of engineers and important to the image of the profession that engineers increase their ability to eloquently articulate the relevance of engineering to many public policy issues. In parallel with this, it is critical to try to improve public understanding of engineering, so that the public can appreciate the value and consequences of new technology and meaningfully participate in public debates where technology is a critical factor.

Attention to ethical issues in engineering through review of case studies—perhaps delivered and supported by advances in information technology (as described in the paper by Donald Falkenburg in Appendix A) will reduce our vulnerability to repeat the mistakes of the past and increase our opportunities to emulate "best practice" successes.

REFERENCES

CABTH (California Business, Transportation, and Housing Agency). 2001. Invest for California: Strategic Planning for California's Future Prosperity and Quality of Life. Report of the California Business, Transportation, and Housing Agency Commission on Building for the 21st Century. Sacramento, Calif. Available online at *http://www.bth.ca.gov/invest4cal*. Accessed May 5, 2005.

CIA (Central Intelligence Agency). 2001. Long-Term Global Demographic Trends: Reshaping the Geopolitical Landscape. Available online at *http://www.odci.gov/cia/reports/Demo_Trends_For_Web.pdf*. Accessed April 19, 2005.

Hinrichsen, D., B. Robey, and U. D. Upadhyay. 1997. Solutions for a Water-Short World. Population Reports, Series M, No. 14. Baltimore, Md.: Population Information Program, Johns Hopkins School of Public Health.

USCB (U.S. Census Bureau). 2002. U.S. Census Bureau National Population Projections. Available online at *http://www.census.gov/population/www/projections/natproj.html*. Accessed April 19, 2005.

Wind, J., and A. Rangaswamy. 2000. *Customerization: The Next Revolution in Mass Customization*. University Park, Pa.: eBusiness Research Center, Pennsylvania State University. Available online at *http://www.smeal.psu.edu/ebrc/publications/res_papers/1999_06.pdf*. Accessed May 5, 2005.

Wright, B. T. 1999. Knowledge Management. Presentation at meeting of Industry–University–Government Roundtable on Enhancing Engineering Education, May 24, 1999, Iowa State University, Ames.

2

The Past as Prologue

In presenting this document for review and use by the community, we recognize that this is not the first time for serious discussions about the character of engineering education in the United States. Some 50 years ago, such debate led to the introduction of the engineering science model of engineering education. It produced engineers who "practiced" differently, and that led to many new products and technologies that were developed more rapidly and were of higher quality than those developed by the semi-empirical methods that were then the norm for engineering practice. Today, the practice of engineering needs to change further because of demands for technologies and products that exceed existing knowledge bases and because of the changing professional environment in which engineers need to operate. That change must be encouraged and facilitated by changes in engineering education, but in contemplating such changes, we are sobered by two realities: first, that scattered interventions across engineering education over the past decade or so have not resulted in systemic change, but rather only in isolated instances of success in individual programs, on individual campuses; and second, that the disconnect between the system of engineering education and the practice of engineering appears to be accelerating. This is due to the explosion of knowledge, the growing complexity and interdependence of societal problems, the worldwide reach of those problems, and the need to operate in a global economy. However, we are optimistic that the community of advocates recognizing the need for change is reaching a critical mass and that coordinated action on a broad scale may be possible and effective.

Efforts to realign engineering education, of varying scopes, have taken place in almost every decade of the twentieth century, beginning in the early 1900s. (See the brief history provided by Bruce Seely in Appendix A.) As a student of this history, Seely suggests points of continuity between this initiative and efforts in past eras, including:

- an explicit desire to increase the public recognition of the role of engineering professionals, to enhance the social status and prestige of the community by depicting a compelling vision of engineering;
- a clear recognition of the need to attract and sustain the interest of students from the groups continually and currently underrepresented in the study and practice of engineering;
- the complex relationship between academic engineering, the corporations and large industrial concerns that employ the great majority of engineering graduates, and the nation's economy;
- a continuous and sometimes contentious debate about the role of liberal studies (humanistic and social science courses) in preparing the professional engineer;
- a persistent struggle to arrive at balance in the several curricular elements in the undergraduate engineering program—the scientific base, the technical core, professional and general education; and
- lurking concerns about institutional inertia, whether in the form of faculty resistance to change or the challenges of moving the "battleship" of the modern research university.

He also suggests that present efforts are characterized by some positive points of departure with past efforts, particularly:

- a motivation to think ahead as a community, to step beyond the immediacy of the moment and the challenges of the present to imagine the future;
- the active engagement of experts from the field of management in the first phase of the Engineer of 2020 Project, informing the process of gathering facts, of forecasting future conditions,

and of developing scenarios of the possible contexts in which the engineer of 2020 will pursue his or her profession;

- a vision that an engineering degree has the potential to become a liberal arts degree for the twenty-first century;
- a realization that the present advocates are perhaps the first generation of reformers to take seriously the opportunity for fashioning a wider portal for engineering, viewing engineering education as concerned with more than the graduation of practicing engineers;
- an undercurrent of awareness that current complexities are so daunting that tinkering at the edges—reforming one course, one program, one department at a time, developing isolated instances of success here and there—is no longer a viable response if we are to build the kind of robust programs in research and education now needed to strengthen the U.S. engineering community by 2020; and
- a recognition that today's concerns extend beyond undergraduate engineering per se, to the interplay of the engineering profession, the practice of engineering, and engineering education as a system.

It is our belief that many, if not all, of these factors are presently in play, which yields a sense of optimism that meaningful reengineering of engineering education can occur in the near future to allow effective preparation of engineering graduates who will be in the most productive phase of their careers in 2020.

3

Getting to 2020: Guiding Strategies

Our goal to ensure effective engineering education should be pursued within the context of a comprehensive examination of all relevant aspects of the interrelated system of systems of engineering education, engineering practice, the K-12 feeder system, and the global economic system. Engineering education must be realigned to promote attainment of the characteristics desired in practicing engineers, and this must be done in the context of an increased emphasis on the research base underlying conduct of engineering practice and engineering education. This will require that action be taken by key stakeholders, particularly engineering faculty and the engineering professional societies.

ENGAGE IN A COMPREHENSIVE EFFORT

Too many efforts at reform attempt to look at single elements of complex interconnected systems. We believe that entire systems must be considered, even if a narrower focus is ultimately taken. Thus, within the context of professional engineering practice, one must consider a system that includes at least the following elements:

- the application of engineering processes to define and solve problems using scientific, technical, and professional knowledge bases;

- engagement of the engineer and professionals from different disciplines in team-based problem-solving processes;
- the tools used by the engineer and other technical professionals;
- interaction of the engineer with the customer and engineering managers to set agreed-upon goals; and
- the economic, political, ethical, and social constraints as boundary conditions that define the possible range of solutions for engineering problems and demand the interaction of engineers with the public.

Similarly, one must consider the several elements of the engineering education system, to include:

- the teaching, learning, and assessment processes that move a student from one state of knowledge and professional preparation to another state;
- students and teachers/faculty as the primary actors within the learning process;
- curricula, laboratories, instructional technologies, and other tools for teaching and learning;
- the goals and objectives of teachers/faculty, departments, colleges, accreditors, employers, and other stakeholders of engineering education;
- the external environment that shapes the overall demand for engineering education (e.g., the business cycle and technological progress); and
- a process for revising goals and objectives as technological advances and other changes occur.

Our goal is to reengineer engineering education. This reengineering focuses not on the enterprise's organization, but on its products and services—in the present case, what higher education would define as its outcomes. Reengineering involves asking the questions: How can we make our processes more effective, more quality conscious, more flexible, simpler, and less expensive? It begins by identifying the desired outcome, product, or service, and then designing backward, using as design criteria what the outcome is supposed to look like and the nature of the processes used to produce it. Quality is measured in terms of both the product (Did we meet our specifications?) and the process (Is it simple, integrated, efficient?). The desired outcomes should include an enhanced educational experience for engineering students, opportunities to pursue engineering as a liberal education, and, in the systems context, program changes and/or efforts by engineering educators that engage and support K-12 faculty, enhance public understanding of engineering, foster technological literacy of the public, and elevate the stature of the profession.

Two recent efforts at comprehensive innovation in engineering education are those launched by the National Science Foundation (NSF) Engineering Education Coalitions (EECs; SRI International, 2000) and the revision of the Engineering Accreditation Criteria by ABET, Inc. (ABET, 2004b). The EECs addressed program structure, curricular content, and pedagogy. Formal evaluations of the various coalitions have been mixed to negative in their judgments of their impact and effectiveness, noting in particular the difficulty of achieving large-scale adoption of the new educational materials developed by the EECs. In a sobering observation, given the desire to impact the education of the engineer of 2020, Froyd (see paper in Appendix A) suggests that it might take several decades for an EEC approach to succeed. On the other hand, comments from many participants in the EECs have been much more positive regarding their impact, noting that the EECs catalyzed a number of systemic changes including the early introduction of engineering and engineering design into the freshman/sophomore curriculum at many institutions and the adoption of continual assessment programs at the course, department, and college levels. They also lead to increased involvement of engineering faculty in the education of freshman and sophomore students; the use, for engineering faculty, of new pedagogical modes; and the introduction of programs such as reverse engineering or dissection.

With regard to ABET, it is noted that, in addition to addressing the traditional educational topics, the revised criteria place particular emphasis on the stakeholder goals and objectives as reflected in the institutional mission. ABET (2004a) also has recently begun exploring the role of accreditation in preparing engineers for working in diverse environments. However, ABET prohibits the accreditation of both a baccalaureate degree and a master's degree in engineering programs with the same name. ABET should revisit this prohibition.

CONSIDER THE LINKAGES

The nature of engineering practice (e.g., the limited contact of most engineers with the public), the credentials required of engineering practitioners, and the structure and rigor of an engineering education vis-à-vis other baccalaureate or professional education programs all play a role in how the public perceives the status (or perceived status) of the engineering profession and individual engineers. In thinking about changes in engineering education, one should think about optimization in a systems sense, to include, for example, how the changes can enhance the stature of the profession.

Science had its origins in the work of scholars supported by wealthy patrons and in the personal work of wealthy aristocrats who looked to the stars to understand the origins of the universe and life or who were intrigued to understand the natural physical, chemical, or biological world around them. Engineering had its origins in the trades, in the effort to make and implement something useful, first for military purposes and later for civil purposes. The artifacts created, deployed, and repaired were made by craftsmen in military armories or tradesmen for the public, and the knowledge to do so was passed from generation to generation by an apprentice system. The forebears of the professional engineering societies were guilds designed to support and preserve this labor system. Although the artifacts produced, such as steam engines, rapidly became more complex than the output of the simple trades and required "engineers" to design and produce them, in some respects it has never been possible to dispel the notion that an engineer is but a highly trained tradesman. Indeed, today there are highly skilled technicians that maintain boilers, sanitation systems, and so on, who are commonly referred to as engineers and have no need of the science and mathematics education of the current engineering baccalaureate degree.

Formal engineering education eventually replaced the apprentice system and, early on, was based on engineering practice. With the increasing complexity of engineering problems, the basis of engineering education shifted to the fundamentals of science and mathematics (in the middle of the twentieth century in the United States). This led to engineers who were more capable and flexible and more able to bring better products to market more quickly, thereby immeasurably improving the standard of engineering practice. As time has progressed, however, a disconnect between engineers in practice and engineers in academe has developed and grown. The great majority of engineering faculty, for example, have no industry experience. Industry representatives point to this disconnect as the reason that engineering students are not adequately prepared, in their view, to enter today's workforce.

It is noteworthy that, for over a century, engineering has adhered to the notion that four years of education is all that is needed to become an engineer. Perhaps reflecting its apprenticeship origins, engineering education appears designed to get graduates into gainful employment, primarily in industry, as fast as possible.[1] Other professions have recognized the inadequacy of this approach (see Figure 3-1). Indeed, because of the educational practice in those professions, there is a perception that one becomes a "professional" following two, three, or more years of education beyond the baccalaureate degree, which is the degree most engineers hold. Thus, it is not so surprising, perhaps, that engineers do not feel that the public values their "professional" status. To this point, data collected for the American Association of Engineering Societies by Harris Interactive (NAE, 2002, p. 11) indicate that scientists continue to be held in higher regard than engineers. In a survey, 55 percent of respondents indicated that scientists had "very great prestige," whereas 34 percent indicated the same for engineers. This level of appreciation for engineers was constant from 1977 to 1998, a performance that Harris rated as "consistently mediocre." Engineers in academe enjoy the personal and professional prestige of their academic environment (in the same 1998 Harris Poll, educators labeled as "teachers" rated at 53 percent), so the prestige of the engineering profession may have a less visceral concern for them, but they can and should play a role in designing an engineering education infrastructure that will enhance the prestige of the profession.

The professional engineering societies addressed this problem early on by creating "professional" engineers who are licensed by examination. This was largely the outgrowth of civil engineering and reflects a need for the public to know whether an engineer they are dealing with on a project is competent. However, with the rise of large corporations, who felt capable of judging competence for themselves and who were

---

[1]The data show that almost 85 percent of baccalaureate recipients are employed by private, for-profit firms. See Table 4 in *http://www.nsf.gov/sbe/srs/infbrief/nsf04316/start.htm*.

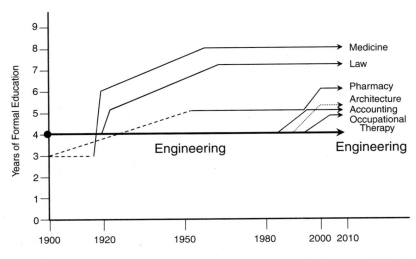

FIGURE 3-1 Years of formal postsecondary education required to begin practicing in different fields. SOURCE: Russell et al. (2001).

more than willing to employ unlicensed engineers and train them in the specific needs of their business, the bachelor's degree became and remains the overwhelmingly dominant ticket for practicing engineering.

It is unreasonable to expect that corporations will require more than a four-year engineering degree for entry-level employment, and thus it is unreasonable to expect that engineering schools will only graduate five-year (or more) degree students. If, as in the past, some schools move to a mandatory five-year program, students will flock to those schools that do not. Similarly, it is unreasonable to expect that professional licensure requirements will change in some way to become attractive to most baccalaureate engineers. Thus, other things being equal, we believe that engineering schools and professional societies need to look to other ways that reinvention of engineering education can enhance the perception of engineering as a profession. A possible alternative is the master's degree, in particular, one that can be designed to be accredited and universally recognized and promoted by both schools and societies as a "professional" degree, perhaps along the lines of a more technology-based MBA. That degree will clearly have to provide value in the marketplace if large numbers of engineers are likely to commit to the time and expense to acquire it.

FOCUS ON LEVERS FOR CHANGE

A factor underlying the systems of engineering practice and engineering education is that the engineering profession has a trans-organizational character. That is, practicing engineers seek to maintain a professional identity that they can carry with them, irrespective of who is their current employer. Membership in professional societies and adherence to professional codes of ethics codified by such societies provide a means to achieve these ends. Professional societies are seen as the primary avenues through which engineers support their identities as professionals, identify opportunities for continuing professional education, and collectively communicate their views on issues affecting their profession to the policy community (Denning, 2001). Professional societies are also key portals through which knowledge is diffused to members of a profession (Hall, 2003). It is through this close connection to their members that professional societies can play an important role in advising on changes in the engineering education system.

Engineering faculty, of course, will be on the front line of any change, and encouraging and enlisting their support for engineering education innovations is essential. Providing incentives for their support is challenged by the present faculty reward system, which bases decisions for tenure primarily on excellence in research. The nation has benefited enormously from the efforts of research universities, through their research faculty and Ph.D. programs, but this has not necessarily translated into excellence in undergraduate education. In a 1998 study, fully 98 percent of students switching from engineering to another major cited poor teaching as a major reason for their departure; 81 percent cited inadequate advising (Adelman, 1998). Thus, increased attention to teaching, to how students learn, and to student mentoring is important for enriching the undergraduate experience. To effect such changes, one must engage engineering faculty leaders, including deans, department chairs, and individual faculty in consideration of how to reward attention to and excellence in such activities.

The other major players in the engineering education system are, of course, the students, who are the "consumers" seeking preparation to enter the profession and, in some sense, are the "products" of the educational system. As consumers, students should be participants in the educational processes. Much has been written about the responsibility that students need to take for their own education and careers. Efforts to help them do so, however, frequently devolve to attempts to "fix" their skills and habits so that they can work within existing systems rather than fixing the systems. Students have a role to play, but fixing the system is not a problem solely, or even primarily, within their domain to correct.

In addition to engaging these "direct" levers for change, the impact of the Engineer of 2020 initiative will also depend on how well it engages the perspectives, imagination, and energies of the broader spectrum of persons who can help in designing, implementing, and assessing systemic change to create an American engineering enterprise in 2020 that will truly serve the interests of society. These include young people who are the rising engineering leaders; those responsible for career development in industry and government; practitioners from multiple disciplines and fields of inquiry beyond engineering; experts in learning theory and colleagues from the learning sciences; those with professional expertise in fields of ethics, communication, and leadership theory; iconoclasts within and beyond engineering, skeptical about the potential of technologies; and those pioneers already mounting programs to change the profession, the practice of engineering, and the environment in which students discover the essence of engineering and are motivated to become engineers.

PURSUE STUDENT-CENTERED EDUCATION

One should address how students learn as well as what they learn in order to ensure that student learning outcomes focus on the performance characteristics needed in future engineers. Two major tasks define this focus: (1) better alignment of engineering curricula and the nature of academic experiences with the challenges and opportunities graduates will face in the workplace and (2) better alignment of faculty skill sets with those needed to deliver the desired curriculum in light of the different learning styles of students.

Engineering professional societies have recognized this challenge and are actively engaged in efforts to create better alignment between academic experiences and anticipated future workplace requirements. For example, various engineering societies are revisiting the bodies of knowledge that should be expected of professionals in their disciplines, including civil (ASCE, 2004) and chemical engineering (Lidtke et al., 2004), computer engineering (IEEE, 2004), and mechanical engineering (Laity, 2004). Engineering professional societies and university faculty also have come together recently to improve the quality and effectiveness of instruction and student learning. The American Institute of Chemical Engineers, the American Society of Civil Engineers, the American Society of Mechanical Engineers, and the Institute of Electrical and Electronics Engineers are collaborating to offer "Excellence in Engineering Education" teaching workshops for engineering faculty.[2]

DEVELOP A RESEARCH BASE

The National Science Board has observed that

> The organizational structures and processes for educating, maintaining skills, and employing science and engineering talent in the workforce are diverse and their interrelationships complex and dynamic. As a result, production and employment of scientists and engineers are not well understood as a system. (NSB, 2003, p. 26)

Moreover, the system is evolving. Rosalyn Williams, historian of science and technology, has asserted that engineering is undergoing a transformative evolution as a profession. The most fundamental engineering processes remain the same (design, development, and so on), but the domains of application are rapidly expanding. We need to develop enhanced understanding of models of engineering practice in this evolving environment (Williams, 2003). The medical community offers an example of the development of such models (Council on Graduate Medical Education, 1999) and nascent efforts exist in the engineering community (see, e.g., description of a seminar sponsored by the University of Western Australia Faculty of Engineering, Computing and Mathematics[3] and Auyang [2004]). Although progress is being made, much remains to be done in developing the research base underlying best practices in engineering education (Wankat et al., 2002) and faculty professional practice generally (Arreola et al., 2003).[4]

---

[2]ExcEED Teaching Workshops for Engineering Faculty. Available online at *http://www.asme.org/education/prodev/teach/*.

[3]Professional Engineering Skills Research. Available online at *http://www.mech.uwa.edu.au/jpt/pes.html*.

[4]Beyond characterizing the system, a key challenge is to understand the roles of the various stakeholders. See Siller and Johnson (2004).

The growing body of research about how students learn can serve as a guide and check at each stage of the work of transforming the undergraduate learning environment. Past attempts toward reforming engineering education—whether in individual courses or programs or on individual campuses—have been informed primarily by the opinions and experiences of those leading these efforts. What "works" has been intuitively felt, rather than based on a body of carefully gathered data that provide evidence of which approaches work for which students in which learning environments. Without such data, engineers, and their colleagues in the scientific community, have found it difficult to evaluate claims, for example, about the effectiveness of emerging pedagogies or the impact of information technologies on strengthening student learning. Unlike the technical community, wherein data-driven results from one lab have widespread impact on the work of peers, many educational reformers have not incorporated research on learning into their work.

The publication of *How People Learn* by the National Research Council (NRC, 1999) was a seminal event in the educational community. It outlined clearly the advances in understanding learning theory achieved by researchers in the learning sciences. Engineering educators should be guided by these findings in order to design and conduct educational research to address critical issues related to broadening participation, improving retention of majors, creating courses for non-majors, and designing an alternative engineering degree for those students interested in careers and public service opportunities outside traditional engineering employment. By focusing on research on learning, we will be able to understand:

- how to serve students with different learning styles;
- why specific approaches and pedagogies work, for example, how research as undergraduates serves learning goals such as personal development, knowledge synthesis, development of skills such as data collection and interpretation, design and hypothesizing, information literacy/computer literacy, and teamwork;
- how to help students clarify, refine, and confirm their career goals and enhance their preparation for career/graduate school, if appropriate;
- how to help them become responsible lifelong learners;
- how information technology can support student learning; and

- how they can best learn the specific skills required for the practice of engineering in the twenty-first century.

COMMUNICATE, COMMUNICATE, COMMUNICATE

A strategy for realigning engineering education must be developed within the contexts of understanding the elements of engineering and recognizing the importance of constant communication with the public and engineering community stakeholders on the goals of education reinvention and the value of success. Communications across the engineering education establishment, which is both a community of common interests and a community of competitors, have been spotty at best, and communications between engineering schools and the public have been lacking as well. The engineering community has shown much interest in enhancing public awareness of engineering and has pursued a wide variety of approaches, including those that communicate to the public the ubiquity of "engineering systems," the role of engineers in the realization of those systems, and the education requirements for such work (NAE, 2002; Constable and Somerville, 2003), but such efforts have not been particularly successful (NAE, 2002). Thus, as noted earlier, the public has little understanding of the nature and value of an engineering education and how changes might make it a more attractive option for their sons and daughters. Communications at both levels must be enhanced as a key element in promoting systemic change of engineering education.

Surveys of precollege students have consistently shown great interest in meaningful career fields tied to "helping others" (Taylor Research & Consulting Group, 2004). Thus, it would be particularly helpful if the engineering community could successfully communicate the social context of engineering—how engineering has made enormous contributions to our quality of life—and the social responsibilities of engineers beyond just taking care to exercise their skills responsibly. Several authors have suggested altering engineering education to explicitly make such connections (COSEPUP, 1995; Schacterle, 1997; Winchester, 1997; Barke et al., 2001). One indication of the failure of the engineering community to communicate this message is provided in Table 3-1, which shows that only 35 percent of college students believe an engineering career is "worth the extra effort." It is both perplexing and disappointing that college students, who presumably have or should have a

TABLE 3-1 Student Perceptions of Professional Careers

Professions	High Opinion, %		Careers "worth the extra effort," %	
	High School Students	College Students	High School Students	College Students
Doctors	78	85	90	92
Lawyers	45	38	71	77
Teachers	66	83	70	81
Engineers	**58**	**72**	**68**	**35**
Accountants/CPA	30	36	40	47

SOURCE: Taylor Research & Consulting Group (2000).

better understanding of the nature of engineering than high school students, have a higher opinion of engineers than high school students have, but are much less likely to believe an engineering career is worth the extra effort.

It is also important for the engineering community to better communicate, in an increasingly technological society, the value of engineering training for a variety of tasks/challenges not typically considered within the boundaries of "traditional" engineering. NSF (1998) data show that there are 2.2 million people with degrees in engineering, and of those, 1.0 million indicate that their principal occupation is not engineering. The value of a broad engineering education, to include, for example, business and communications expertise, for those who aspire to management can be deduced from the NSF data in Figure 3-2, which show that, "among master's-level engineering graduates in the private for-profit sector (where most engineering graduates work), those who have combined their engineering degree(s) with a degree outside science or engineering are more likely to become senior managers (someone responsible for leading others in management) at some point in their career" (NSF, 1998).

Similarly, it is important to help the public understand the breadth of engineering as well as its depth. Many consider engineering to involve, among other things, the application of scientific principles to the solution of human challenges. For a long time the scientific principles of interest were those of the physical sciences. Recent advances in the

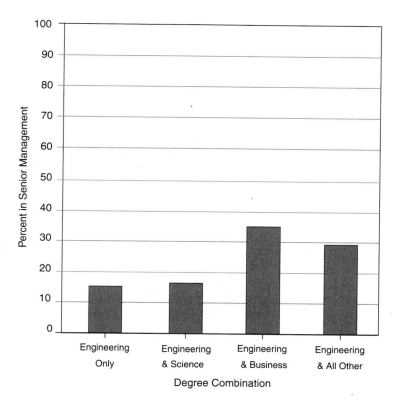

FIGURE 3-2 Likelihood of being in senior management of master's level engineering graduates in the private sector, by degree combination, 1995.
NOTE: Master's degrees may be in any field, any degree combinations imply neither order of degree fields nor number of degrees earned. In this figure, social sciences are included in "other."
SOURCE: NSF (1998).

fields of information technology and the life sciences have led to increasing exploration of engineering as an application of these separate, yet related, sciences. Engineering education options open to students are thus expanding, and communicating the nature of those options is essential to attracting the most talented students.

REFERENCES

ABET, Inc. 2004a. Proceedings of the 2004 ABET Annual Meeting: Competing in a Diverse World. Baltimore, Md.

ABET, Inc. 2004b. Sustaining the Change. Available online at *http://www.abet.org/Linked% 20Documents-UPDATE/White%20Papers/Sustaining%20the%20Change-Web.pdf.* Accessed May 19, 2005.

Adelman, C. 1998. *Women and Men of the Engineering Path: A Model for Analysis of Undergraduate Careers.* Washington, D.C.: U.S. Department of Education.

Arreola, R., M. Theall, and L. Aleamoni. 2003. Beyond Scholarship: Recognizing the Multiple Roles of the Professoriate. Presented at the 2003 American Educational Research Association convention. Available online at *http://www.cedanet.com/meta/Beyond% 20Scholarship.pdf.* Accessed April 19, 2005.

ASCE (American Society of Civil Engineers). 2004. *Civil Engineering Body of Knowledge for the 21st Century.* Reston, Va. Available online at *http://www.asce.org/professional/educ/ bodyofknowledge.cfm.* Accessed April 3, 2005.

Auyang, S. 2004. *Engineering: An Endless Frontier.* Cambridge, Mass.: Harvard University Press. Web site supplement available online at *http://www.creatingtechnology.org/eng.htm.* Accessed July 7, 2005.

Barke, R., E. O. Lane, and K. Knoespel. 2001. Shaping the Future of American University Education. Prepared for the 4th POSTI International Conference, Europe's 21st Century Politics for Sustainable Technological Innovation: The Role of Higher Education in Science, Technology, and Society, May 20-21, Oslo, Norway. Available online at *http://www.esst.uio.no/posti/workshops/barke.pdf.* Accessed July 8, 2005.

Constable, G., and B. Somerville. 2003. *A Century of Innovation: Twenty Engineering Achievements That Transformed Our Lives.* Washington, D.C.: Joseph Henry Press.

COSEPUP (Committee on Science, Engineering, and Public Policy). 1995. *Reshaping the Graduate Education of Scientists and Engineers.* Washington, D.C.: National Academy Press. Available online at *http://books.nap.edu/books/0309052858/html/4.html#pagetop.* Accessed July 8, 2005.

Council on Graduate Medical Education. 1999. *Physician Education for a Changing Healthcare Environment.* Washington, D.C.: U.S. Department of Health and Human Services, Health Resources and Services Administration. Available online at *http:// cogme.gov/13.pdf.* Accessed July 7, 2005.

Denning, P. 2001. "When IT Becomes a Profession." Pp. 295-325 in *The Invisible Future.* New York: McGraw-Hill. Available online at *http://cne.gmu.edu/pjd/PUBS/WhenITProf. pdf.* Accessed May 4, 2005.

Hall, P. 2003. *"A Historical Overview of Philanthropy, Voluntary Associations, and Nonprofit Organizations in the United States, 1600-2000."* In W. W. Powell and R. Steinberg, eds., The Nonprofit Sector: A Research Handbook—Second Edition. New Haven, Conn.: Yale University Press. Available online at *http://ksghome.harvard.edu/~phall/ Powell%20Essay-Final%20-%20rev.pdf.* Accessed April 19, 2005.

IEEE (Institute of Electrical and Electronics Engineers). 2004. A Report on the Model Curriculum for Computer Engineering, Session F3B. Frontiers in Education 34th Annual Conference. Available online at *http://fie.engrng.pitt.edu/fie2004/papers/1189.pdf].* Accessed April 19, 2005.

Laity, W. 2004. A Vision for the Future of Mechanical Engineering Education. Available online at *http://www.asme.org/education/enged/pdf/vision.pdf.* Accessed April 18, 2005.

Lidtke, D., R. Seagrave, and S. Walesh. 2004. Defining the body of knowledge. *ABET Communications Link* (Fall/Winter 2004): 20–22. Available online at *http://www. abet.org/Linked%20Documents-UPDATE/Newsletters/Fall-Winter-2004.pdf.* Accessed May 19, 2005.

NAE (National Academy of Engineering). 2002. *Raising Public Awareness of Engineering.* Washington, D.C.: The National Academies Press.

NRC (National Research Council). 1999. *How People Learn: Brain, Mind, Experience, and School.* Washington, D.C.: National Academy Press.

NSB (National Science Board). 2003. T*he Science and Engineering Workforce: Realizing America's Potential.* Report 03-69. Arlington, Va.: National Science Foundation. Available online at *http://www.nsf.gov/nsb/documents/2003/nsb0369/nsb0369.pdf.* Accessed July 8, 2005.

NSF (National Science Foundation). 1998. *Degrees and Occupations in Engineering: How Much Do They Diverge?* Science and Engineering Statistics Issue Brief NSF 99-318. Available online at *http://www.nsf.gov/statistics/issuebrf/ib99318.htm.* Accessed July 8, 2005.

Russell, J. S., B. Stouffer, and S. G. Walesh. 2001. Business Case for the Master's Degree: The Financial Side of the Equation. Pp. 49-58 in *Proceedings of the Third National Education Congress, Civil Engineering Education Issues,* D. E. Hancher, ed. Reston, Va.: American Society of Civil Engineers.

Schacterle, L. 1997. A Liberal Education for the 2000's. Presented at the ASEE/IEEE Frontiers in Education Conference. Available online at *http://fie.engrng.pitt.edu/fie97/papers/ 1463.pdf.* Accessed May 4, 2005.

Siller, T. J., and G. R. Johnson. 2004. Constituent Influences on Engineering Curricula. *Proceedings of the 2004 American Society for Engineering Education Annual Conference & Exposition.* Washington, D.C.: American Society for Engineering Education. Available online at *http://www.asee.org/acPapers/2004-1680_Final.pdf.* Accessed July 7, 2005.

SRI International. 2000. Progress of the Engineering Education Coalitions. Prepared for the National Science Foundation. Available online at *http://www.nsf.gov/pubs/2000/ nsf00116/nsf00116.doc.* Accessed July 8, 2005.

Taylor Research & Consulting Group (2004). Student and Academic Research Study: Final Quantitative Study. New York: American Institute of Public Accountants. Available online at *http://www.aicpa.org/members/div/career/edu/taylor.htm.* Accessed July 8, 2005.

Wankat, P. C., R. M. Felder, K. A. Smith, and F. S. Oreovicz. 2002. The Engineering Approach to the Scholarship of Teaching and Learning. Pp. 217-237 in *Disciplinary Styles in the Scholarship of Teaching and Learning: Exploring Common Ground,* M. T. Huber and S. Morreale, eds. Washington, D.C.: American Association for Higher Education. Available online at *http://www.ncsu.edu/felder-public/papers/Scholarship_chapter.pdf.* Accessed July 8, 2005.

Williams, R. 2003. Education for the Profession Formerly Known as Engineering. The Chronicle of Higher Education, Volume 49, Issue 20, p. B12, January 24, 2003. Available online (subscription required) at *http://chronicle.com/weekly/v49/i20/20b01201.htm.* Accessed July 7, 2005.

Winchester, I. 1997. Engineering as a Liberal Art. Presentation to the Schulich School of Engineering, University of Calgary. Available online at *http://www.eng.ucalgary.ca/ dean_series/libart1.htm.* Accessed July 8, 2005.

4

Guideposts to the Future

There are a variety of mechanisms and specific programs that have been investigated and/or developed to affect changes in education in general, and engineering education in particular. Some examples of these are discussed below.

COLLABORATIONS

The difficulty of effecting change duly noted, there are, perhaps, some advantages now over past attempts to transform undergraduate engineering. For example, there is a wide range of collaborations already in place—some sponsored by federal agencies such as the National Science Foundation (NSF); others sparked by industry, foundations, and/or professional associations; and others engaging global partners. These collaborations demonstrate that there are effective means for building the kinds of formal and informal relationships needed to effect systemic change. From these collaborations, we can learn about the processes of collective goal setting; of designing, implementing, and assessing curricular and pedagogical approaches; and of using technologies to enhance learning. There are also lessons learned about how to, or how not to, adapt innovations and reforms in different settings, on campuses with different missions and circumstances. The experiences of departments and institutions involved in the NSF-funded Engineering Coalitions, the most recent Grand Challenges effort, and in the

Whitaker Foundation-funded development of biomedical engineering programs, as well as efforts on individual campuses exploring the wide range of experimentation enabled by ABET and its accreditation criteria, must be captured, distilled, and disseminated as "lessons learned" to the broader community. Where those efforts have had mostly local impact, the challenge is to promulgate their successes to other locales and, where appropriate, to coalesce their efforts on a national scale.

The Engineer of 2020 initiative does not assume that there is one right way to transform the learning environment; we recognize that we must understand and capitalize on the treasure that is the diversity of American higher education. Through this initiative, by 2020, engineering programs across the country might be designed for specific areas of distinction, perhaps serving the regional industrial community, perhaps linking to institutional objectives to infuse a global dimension into the undergraduate learning environment, perhaps focusing on a particular thrust within engineering, and/or spotlighting the development of leaders for the engineering profession. We recognize that support will be needed at the local level for adapting the work of others; that campus leaders must exercise leadership to shape an agenda for action that makes sense for them, given their mission, circumstances, and vision of the future. Success will require asking the right questions at each stage of the process and continually revisiting those questions in the context of the answers returned—creating, articulating, and driving a vision to implementation.

TECHNOLOGIES FOR COLLABORATION

In addition to the experience of many active collaborations, another significant advantage over past efforts is in the electronic technologies that enable sharing of ideas, materials, and other resources relating to the transformation of individual courses or labs, departments, programs, or institutions. It will be important to approach this sharing of information systematically, integrating the identification, analysis, and dissemination of appropriate data and best practices into each stage of course, curriculum, and laboratory transformation.

RELATED EFFORTS

A fortuitous leverage point for realizing our goals to reengineer undergraduate engineering by 2020 is that the engineering community can learn from the experiences of individuals and institutions working to transform undergraduate programs, within and beyond STEM (science, technology, engineering, and mathematics). Leaders in other sectors, professions, and disciplines are similarly examining societal and educational trends that affect learning in their fields. The undergraduate physics community, for one, has worked for decades to establish goals for student learning and to develop inventories that monitor progress toward realizing those goals in individual classes, programs, and departments.[1] So, collaborations within a campus—across disciplinary boundaries, engaging pedagogical pioneers—extend opportunities for sharing best practices beyond the community of engineering educators, for learning what works, for example, in building interdisciplinary teams, in serving students from groups currently underrepresented in the study and practice of STEM fields, and in bringing real-world concerns into a discovery-based learning environment.

STEM fields are all dealing with the same trends that are redefining the undergraduate learning environment, including:

- the awareness that exposure to science, mathematics, technology, and engineering during their undergraduate career is good preparation for a "wide variety of societal roles; and that the nation will depend increasingly on a citizenry with a solid base of scientific and technical understanding" (Center for Science, Mathematics, and Engineering Education, 1996, p. 4);
- the momentum toward integrating research and education so that all students have access to discovery-based, problem-solving learning experiences;

---

[1]The Force Concept Inventory (FCI) is described by Hestenes et al. (1992) as the set of six Newtonian force concepts that leads to an accurate understanding of force and motion. The FCI explores student conceptual understanding of kinematics, the first, second, and third laws of motion, the superposition principle, and kinds of force by providing questions with a single Newtonian-based answer along with "commonsense" misconceptions that serve as powerful distracters.

- the dissolution of boundaries between disciplines such that "imagination, diversity, and the capacity to adapt quickly have become essential qualities for both institutions and individuals, not only to facilitate research, but also to ensure the immediate and broad-based application of research results related to the environment. To meet these complex challenges as well as urgent human needs, we need to . . . frame integrated interdisciplinary research questions and activities and to merge data, approaches, and ideas across spatial, temporal, and societal scales" (AC-ERE, 2003);

- the efforts of the learning sciences community and researchers in specific disciplines exploring how people learn that are providing a solid theoretical foundation for designing, implementing, and assessing new approaches to transform undergraduate education—course by course and program by program, as well as at the institution-wide level—to enhance student learning (NRC, 1999);

- external pressures for accountability that call for greater stewardship over the quality and character of learning—requiring a clearly defined mission, explicit educational goals, and documented progress toward meeting those goals (ABET, 2005, p. 1);

- student demographics, with greater diversity from the perspectives of academic preparation, career aspirations, and ethnic background that require approaches to learning, teaching, and research designed intentionally to respect (and celebrate) this diversity;

- faculty demographics—a pattern of heavy retirements now underway and anticipated in the immediate future affords an opportunity to reconsider preparation of incoming faculty, including consideration of what kinds of skills they will need and what rewards and incentives will be offered for their scholarly efforts;

- economic pressures to use resources as efficiently as possible to serve agreed-upon priorities; and

- opportunities afforded by new technologies to transform the learning environment:

Powerful new technologies now under development by U.S. businesses, universities, and government promise to transform virtually every industry and many human endeavors. These technologies could possibly also be harnessed to transform education and training in ways previously unimaginable. Rapid advancements in the years ahead could enable new learning environments using simulations, visualizations, immersive environments, game playing, intelligent tutors and avatars, networks of learning, reusable building blocks of content, and more. The technologies that are coming could create rich and compelling learning opportunities that meet all learners' needs, and provide knowledge and training when and where it is needed, while boosting the productivity of learning and lowering its cost. (Evans, 2002, p. ii)

SPECIFIC PROGRAMS AND MECHANISMS

The discussions presented under this heading are intended to present some examples of efforts to improve engineering education, not a comprehensive review. In the context of thinking of engineering as a system of systems, it provides examples related to K-12 preparation, increasing retention in engineering programs, attracting students from underrepresented groups, entrepreneurship, technology-enabled learning, program flexibility, reconsidering what an "engineering education" means, and preparation of engineering faculty. Although most of these examples deal with the "efficiency" and "throughput" of engineering education, these approaches also serve to develop skills that industry has repeatedly stated are necessary for performing well.

The K-12 System and Engineering Education

Several individuals commented at the summit that the current K-12 system does not provide a sufficiently rigorous education to large numbers of students, particularly in the inner-city schools, to allow them to enter and succeed in an engineering program. As a community, engineering educators are working to assist the K-12 community to understand the engineering profession and how engineering activities can invigorate the teaching of mathematics and science in the K-12 classrooms. Many programs are actively engaging K-12 districts and faculty across the country; however, there are several that stand out with respect to their growth in number of schools, connection to state education standards, and support from stakeholders. Following is a brief description of some of these notable programs:

Project Lead the Way (PLTW) was initiated by Richard Blais in the 1980s while he was chairman of the technology department of an upstate New York school district. Partnerships with private philanthropy and the Rochester Institute of Technology (the program's first national training center) allowed the program to grow into a national organization with 22 institutions of higher education supporting schools in over 40 states that institute some or all of PLTW's middle school and high school curricula of hands-on, problem-based, technology-driven learning.[2]

The *Infinity Project* was developed in the late 1990s by a national team of engineering educators led by Geoffrey Orsak at Southern Methodist University that had as its goal to help "students see the real value of math and science and its varied applications to high-tech engineering."[3] With strong support from Texas Instruments and state and national government, the Infinity curriculum has demonstrated tremendous growth in Texas high schools and is in place in 80 schools in 21 other states.[4] Precourse and postcourse surveys of student attitudes have shown a significant growth in student interest in pursuing an engineering degree, with nearly 80 percent of students indicating a "very strong interest" in pursuing engineering.[5]

Massachusetts K-12 Engineering Standards were instituted in 2001 and provide K-12 educators with guidelines for age-appropriate inquiry-based learning. The frameworks also provide students with an introduction into the ways in which engineering/technology is related to, but substantially different from, the field of science—"Technology/engineering seeks different ends from those of science." The outcomes of science

---

[2]See *http://www.pltw.org/AUHistory.shtml and http://www.pltw.org/network.shtml.*
[3]See *http://www.infinity-project.org.*
[4]See *http://www.infinity-project.org/infinity/infinity_outcome.html.*
[5]See *http://www.infinity-project.org/files/infinity_powerpoint.ppt#275,20,Student%20 Impact.*

can be defined simplistically as observation, experimentation, and documentation that allows for generalized statements concerning patterns in nature. Conversely, "engineering strives to design and manufacture useful devices or materials, defined as technologies, whose purpose is to increase our efficacy in the world and/or our enjoyment of it" (Massachusetts Department of Education, 2001, p. 3).

NSF is supporting the development of the National Science Digital Library (NSDL) to provide "educational resources for science, technology, engineering and mathematics education."[6] One of the collections being funded through the NSDL program is called *TeachEngineering.com*. This collaboration consists of engineering educators at several Research-Extensive[7] institutions that were previously awarded grants in NSF's Graduate Teaching Fellows in K-12 Education program.[8] The project brings together the knowledge and content created by these separate efforts, gives the content materials a "common look and feel," and provides a system architecture that allows K-12 teachers to search the collection in a variety of ways (subject matter, content domain, grade level, national standards, and selected state standards). The goal of *TeachEngineering* is to rapidly build on the number of curricular units in the collection and to map all content to standards of all 50 states.[9]

These efforts and others represent real progress in changing the public understanding of engineering and should, over time, begin to enhance the recruitment of students into engineering who are knowledgeable of the field and prepared academically for its rigors. The goal for higher education is to connect these students to a curriculum that is challenging, exciting, and relevant to student interests. Summit attendees advocated for a curriculum designed around grand challenges that would serve to engage and inspire students in a way that makes the engineer's contribution to society more explicit.

---

[6]See *http://www.nsdl.org/about/*.

[7]These institutions typically offer a wide range of baccalaureate programs, and they are committed to graduate education through the doctorate. During the period studied, they awarded 50 or more doctoral degrees per year across at least 15 disciplines. From *http://www.carnegiefoundation.org/Classification/CIHE2000/defNotes/Definitions.htm*.

[8]A description and solicitation are available online at *http://www.nsf.gov/funding/pgm_summ.jsp?pims_id=5472&from=fund*.

[9]Jacquelyn Sullivan, Lead Principal Investigator of TeachEngineering.com, personal communication, January 4, 2005.

Retention

The ABET EC2000 criteria (ABET, 2005) and the Engineer of 2020 Phase I Report (NAE, 2004) reflect a desire to produce engineers with technical competence and a broader array of "professional skills" than the traditional curriculum seeks to develop. At the same time, engineering educators and American industry have been working to create systems that lead to improved retention of students and broader participation of women and minorities. Fortunately, these goals are not incompatible with one another, and institutions have experimented with a variety of approaches to realign the traditional curriculum and to enhance student support mechanisms to meet them. Some notable examples are briefly described below.

Only 40 to 60 percent of entering engineering students persist to an engineering degree, and women and minorities are at the low end of that range. These retention rates represent an unacceptable systemic failure to support student learning in the field. (See Bennett Stewart's comments in Appendix B; also see Seymour and Hewitt, 1997.) To address this issue, it is becoming increasingly recognized that it is important to introduce engineering activities, including team-based design projects and community service projects, early in the undergraduate experience alongside basic science and math courses, so that students begin to develop an understanding of the essence of engineering as early as possible. For example, the impact on retention of a First Year Engineering Projects (FYEP) course was documented by Knight et al. (2003) of the University of Colorado at Boulder and is summarized in Figure 4-1.

One of the earliest curricular interventions to introduce engineering activities at the beginning of the curriculum was led by Eli Fromm of Drexel University. Working with a team that encompassed faculty members from across the entire institution, the new college of engineering curriculum was "organized into four interwoven sequences replacing and/or integrating material from 37 existing courses in the university's traditional lower division curriculum" (Fromm, 2002). These vertically integrated sequences, which included substantial early engineering laboratory experiences, resulted in improved retention (21 percent increase) of students in the trial cohort and an even greater increase in the rate of on-time graduation (50 percent increase). The Drexel curricular approach was successfully replicated by the Gateway Coalition members during the 1990s.

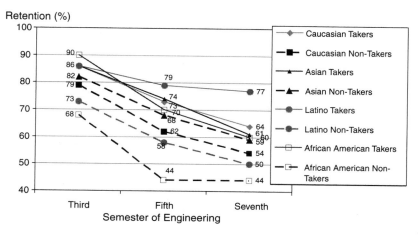

FIGURE 4-1 Long-term retention rates of students taking freshman design course ("Takers") compared to students that did not ("Non-Takers"). The data total 2,581 students with 1,035 students who took the FYEP course and 1,546 students who did not take the course. The sample includes 2,057 men and 524 women with 2,063 Caucasian students (80%), 190 Asian students (7.4%), 160 Latino students (6.2%), and 35 African American students (1.4%). SOURCE: Knight et al. (2003).

An example of a scheme for introducing design activities is illustrated by the curriculum of Olin College of Engineering (see paper by Kerns et al. in Appendix A), which was developed by the faculty with feedback from a cohort of 30 students who were part of Olin's initial class. The system that Olin's faculty developed includes roughly 20 percent design activities in the first year, with the design tasks constructed in such a way that deep content knowledge of materials/engineering principles is less necessary than use of tools (software packages, rapid prototyping equipment) and the application of creativity. By the final year, students are engaged in design activities roughly 80 percent of the time, and greater content knowledge is expected. Note that these design experiences are in both team and individual settings and that students are often responsible for self-directed learning—and teaching their fellow students—in areas that will support a more effective and innovative design solution.

A separate approach to introducing design into the curriculum is modeled by what is known as "service learning" or "experiential learning." The Engineering Projects in Community Service (EPICS) program at Purdue has shown tremendous success in its 10 years of existence. EPICS projects are designed to engage students from engineering and other disciplines in activities to support community-based organizations that serve community needs in social services, education, and the environment. These projects, which can begin in the freshman year and may continue to graduation, allow students to design, build, deploy, and maintain engineered solutions in response to customer needs. By engaging with the community, students quickly understand how engineers contribute to society and learn how the scientific and technical courses they are taking contribute to innovative solutions to real-world challenges. In the process, students strengthen skills related to customer relations, problem analysis and definition, communication, teamwork, and designing/building/testing their solutions.[10] Industry has recognized the promise of the EPICS approach by supporting new EPICS programs at seven institutions nationally, and members of the NSF-sponsored Corporate and Foundation Alliance have partnered with the NSF Division of Engineering Education and Centers to foster the spread of service learning as a means to broaden participation and increase retention.[11]

Specifically regarding the low retention rates (and low enrollment) of women in engineering programs, the NSF Women's Experiences in College Engineering Project conducted extensive data-gathering surveys of students, administrators, and faculty to determine the program components and support mechanisms that produce higher retention rates. Early exposure to the design, build, and test process that marks the practice of engineering was found to be important. Additionally, those who persist in engineering point to such positive factors as Women in Engineering programs, woman-only courses that teach skills such as tool use and computer graphics that help bridge some skill gaps, and advisors—particularly in freshman and sophomore years—who help to provide information, encouragement, and a welcoming environment (Goodman et al., 2002).

---

[10]See *http://epics.ecn.purdue.edu/*.
[11]See *http://www.cfalliance.org/history.html*.

Diversity

In her comments at the summit, Shirley Ann Jackson stressed the need to broaden the participation of underrepresented minorities in engineering and cited a BEST (2004) report that examined programs across the country that have been working to increase diversity in STEM fields and recognized that there were common characteristics at successful institutions. These characteristics are summarized in Table 4-1.

A particular example of a program to increase diversity is one developed by the Georgia Institute of Technology (May and Chubin, 2003). In cooperation with historically black colleges and universities (HBCU) in the Atlanta area, Georgia Tech has created a dual-degree engineering program that is graduating 30 to 40 African American engineers per year out of a total of about 130 African American engineering graduates each year (best in the United States for a non-HBCU). Another program is the partnership between the University of California at Los Angeles (UCLA) and the Hewlett-Packard (HP) Company to deploy

TABLE 4-1 Design Principles to Expand Higher Education Capacity

Principle	Evidence
Institutional leadership	Commitment to inclusiveness across the campus community
Targeted recruitment	Investing in and executing a feeder system, K-12
Engaged faculty	Developing student talent as a rewarded faculty outcome
Personal attention	Addressing, through mentoring and tutoring, the learning needs of each student
Peer support	Providing student interaction opportunities that build support across cohorts and allegiance to institution, discipline, and profession
Enriched research	Providing beyond-the-classroom hands-on opportunities and summer internships that connect experience to the world of work
Bridging to the next level	Building institutional relationships that help students and faculty to envision pathways to milestones and career development
Continuous evaluation	Ongoing monitoring of process and outcomes that guide program adjustments to heighten impact

the Diversity in Education Initiative in the city of Los Angeles.[12] Led by the staff of the Center for Excellence in Engineering and Diversity, UCLA faculty engaged with the K-12 system in urban Los Angeles to build capacity of math and science educators in order to better prepare a greater number of minority students. The top students from these school districts are eligible for 1 of 10 HP scholarships that provide the students with tuition money, computer equipment, summer internships, and an industry mentor. The program has experienced great success in the early years with marked increases in advanced placement course enrollments in high school, a greater number of engineering/computer science–ready high school graduates, and higher retention for the HP scholars in engineering and computer science majors.

Skill Development—Preparing for Rapid Technological Change

In addition to developing the FYEP courses, Jacquelyn Sullivan and L. E. Carlson have utilized the Integrated Teaching and Learning Laboratory at the University of Colorado at Boulder to develop a course called "Innovation and Invention" that introduces students to entrepreneurial pursuits while building strong interdisciplinary and team skills. As Nicholas Donofrio described while addressing the summit, "Invention alone does not guarantee value. That's where innovation comes in. It is the *application of invention*—the fusion of new developments and new approaches to solve real problems." These types of entrepreneurial courses were widely supported by industry representatives at the 2020 Summit, and the entrepreneurial/innovator role was viewed as a unique American strength that should be supported in view of increasing global competition. Recognizing that "inventors frequently depend on a mix of deep theoretical understanding of materials and processes and hands-on experiential knowledge of how things work in the physical and social worlds," courses such as Innovation and Invention begin to develop the boundary-broaching skills that typically mark the innovator (Committee for Study of Invention, 2004). Other professional skills that are realized in a course of this type relate to communication skills because students must present and defend product design features and work closely with peers (from engineering, business, and other domains) and advisors.

---

[12]See *http://www.cfalliance.org/gallery.html.*

Technology-Enabled Learning—
Modularity and Lifelong Learning

The use of information technology-enabled learning (TEL) is in its early stages (see Falkenburg's paper in Appendix A). An example of TEL is the Laboratory for Innovative Technology and Engineering Education (LITEE) project headquartered at Auburn University. LITEE educators have worked with industry partners to develop a series of case studies—delivered through CD-ROM "textbooks," which include video and audio clips, data sets, photographs, drawings, and animations that the students choose how to unpack—that deal with current issues related to design for safety, B2B e-commerce, new product research and design, and the impact of engineering analysis on economic outcomes.[13] Rigorous evaluation of the LITEE project has shown how these technology-enabled cases positively influence persistence in engineering, development of higher order cognitive skills, improved communication and teamwork skills, and a better understanding of the practice of engineering.

One of the discussion threads of the summit breakouts dealt with the short "shelf life" of knowledge in today's world (and what shelf life might be in 2020). It was asserted that students need to develop the skills and attitudes that foster lifelong learning and that technology advances that allow distance and asynchronous learning could be key enablers to support that learning. The Massachusetts Institute of Technology Open Courseware initiative is probably among the best-known efforts with respect to providing access to engineering content, and the leadership of the institution should be commended for this bold initiative. However, content is only a small part of the technology-enabled/lifelong-learning puzzle. Research on Web-mediated learning must continue so that we can better understand how to utilize the electronic multimedia approaches to teaching and learning with respect to engineering content knowledge.

---

[13]See *http://www.auburn.edu/research/litee/casestudy/index.html.* Accessed July 9, 2005.

Program Flexibility

Reports from the National Center for Educational Statistics (Adelman, 1999) and the American Association of Colleges and Universities (AAC&U, 2002) document the rising numbers of students who already attend more than one institution during the course of their undergraduate studies—a course-taking strategy sometimes referred to as "swirling." We simply note that there are many commendable examples of articulation agreements that are arranged between two-year and four-year institutions that facilitate the transition across that interface.

Summit participants did question what needs to occur to construct an even more flexible degree path for students, for example, for a student to concurrently enroll in calculus courses online from a for-profit provider, to take physics at the local community college, to take management courses at a liberal arts college and engineering courses at a research institution. Such an education path would clearly represent a challenge of integration, and research and development of robust assessment tools would be necessary to ensure degree quality.

An Alternative Engineering Degree

In one of the Summit breakout groups, the central topic of discussion was the concept of engineering becoming a "liberal arts degree" for the twenty-first century. The traditional liberal arts degree was characterized as providing the knowledge, skills, and breadth of thinking necessary to perform in leadership roles in government, industry, and, more broadly, all aspects of society. As our everyday life becomes more driven by technology and the panoply of decisions that we must make regarding the use (or rejection) of technological solutions, understanding of the "engineering approach" should likewise become more valued to all well-informed citizens. In that regard, Summit participants from Lafayette College and Princeton University discussed how their institutions have developed bachelor of arts degrees for engineering that are intended to appeal to a broader (or alternative) set of students than the bachelor of science (B.S.) degree. In the case of Lafayette, the curriculum for the first-year bachelor of arts (B.A.) student matches that of the B.S. student; in succeeding years, the B.A. student chooses from a broader set of electives in economics, management, and the liberal arts. The faculty views the B.A. in engineering as the liberal arts degree for the technological age—preparing students for careers in manufacturing, management, finance, or government.[14] Other institutions, for example, Columbia University in New York, have created "3/2 Plans" that combine three years of study in the liberal arts and two years of engineering study that result in students earning two degrees (a B.A. in liberal arts and a B.S. in engineering).[15]

Downey and Lucena (1998) contend that there can be multiple engineering tracks that serve different end purposes for different students. For example, there can be an engineering sciences track, an engineering management track, a public policy track, and an engineering design track. These multiple tracks could serve as a recruiting tool and strengthen the baccalaureate engineering degree into what Carmi and Aung (1993) refer to as the "optimum launch pad to challenging and rewarding professions—engineering first and foremost, but also medicine, law and business."

We recognize that not every institution with an engineering program will be able to or will want to create these different tracks; however, graduates from such programs could provide an infusion of engineering awareness and habits of mind that would serve to strengthen technological literacy in both the public and private sectors.

Faculty Development

The examples described above cannot be successfully adapted and adopted (nor, for that matter, will new approaches be developed) if future faculty are not exposed to the challenges of teaching during their postgraduate studies, or if current faculty are not actively encouraged and supported to develop their skills as teachers. There has been substantial activity in faculty development in areas of pedagogy and assessment, such as in NSF's Preparing Future Faculty program that funded work by the Council of Graduate Schools and the AAC&U. The goal of these programs is to better prepare graduate students for the role of educator that they will be expected to fill following their advanced degree. NSF and other agencies also fund a variety of faculty development

---

[14]See *http://www.lafayette.edu/admissions/majors/ba_engineering.html#course.*
[15]See *http://www.engineering.columbia.edu/admissions/cp/.*

workshops that have demonstrated success. The Carnegie Foundation for the Advancement of Teaching is in the process of evaluating the preparation of engineering faculty as one part of their Preparation for the Professions Program (see paper by Sheppard, Sullivan, and Colby in Appendix A; see also Davidson and Ambrose, 1994). In the study, investigators have identified three "signature pedagogies" in engineering and will seek to determine "their power in fostering a particular kind of learning, their limitations, and creative approaches to overcoming those limitations." However, Summit participants voiced the desire for a more uniform approach to developing faculty skills in areas of curriculum development, material development, and pedagogical skills.

The Higher Education Centers for Learning and Teaching may begin to address that desire. Funded by NSF, these centers are engaged in research to develop a better understanding of effective teaching and learning in STEM fields. The centers are intended to provide a broader education research base and to apply that research in order to provide current and future faculty with the sorts of content knowledge and pedagogical skills that lead to improved student learning in STEM disciplines. The collaborative effort known as the Center for the Integration of Research, Teaching, and Learning, located at the University of Wisconsin at Madison (partnering with faculty members at Michigan State University and Pennsylvania State University), seeks to have a national impact by focusing on the roughly 100 research institutions that supply the large majority of faculty to the nearly 4,000 institutions of higher education with STEM programs.[16] The Center for the Advancement of Engineering Education (CAEE)—a collaboration among researchers at the Colorado School of Mines, Howard University, University of Minnesota, Stanford University, and University of Washington (lead)—focuses on the advancement of scholarship in engineering learning and teaching with a goal to inform the practice of engineering teaching. The CAEE effort will also work to "strengthen the research and leadership skills of the engineering faculty and graduate student community."[17]

---

[16]See *http://cirtl.wceruw.org/ourwork_overview.html*.

[17]See *http://www.engr.washington.edu/caee/index.html*.

REFERENCES

AAC&U (American Association of Colleges and Universities). 2002. Greater Expectations: A New Vision for Learning as a Nation Goes to College. National Panel Report. Washington, D.C.: AAC&U. Available online at *http://www.greaterexpectations.org/pdf/ GEX.FINAL.pdf.* Accessed July 9, 2005.

ABET, Inc. 2005. Criteria for Accrediting Engineering Programs. Available online at *http:// www.abet.org/Linked%20Documents-UPDATE/Criteria%20and%20PP/05-06- EAC%20Criteria.pdf.* Accessed July 12, 2005.

AC-ERE (Advisory Committee for Environmental Research and Education). 2003. Complex Environmental Systems: Synthesis for Earth, Life and Society in the 21st Century. Arlington, Va.: National Science Foundation. Available online at *http://www.nsf.gov/ geo/ere/ereweb/ac-ere/acere_synthesis_rpt_full.pdf.* Accessed July 8, 2005.

Adelman, C. 1999. Answers in the Tool Box: Academic Integrity, Attendance Patterns, and Bachelor's Degree Attainment. Jessup, Md.: Education Publications Center, U.S. Department of Education.

BEST (Building Engineering and Science Talent). 2004. A Bridge for All: Higher Education Design Principles to Broaden Participation in Science, Technology, Engineering and Mathematics. San Diego, Calif.: BEST. Available online at *http://www.bestworkforce.org/ PDFdocs/BEST_BridgeforAll_HighEdFINAL.pdf.* Accessed July 9, 2005.

Carmi, S., and W. Aung. 1993. Launching leaders. *ASEE Prism* 2(March):44.

Center for Science, Mathematics, and Engineering Education. 1996. *From Analysis to Action: Undergraduate Education in Science, Mathematics, Engineering, and Technology.* Washington, D.C.: National Academy Press.

Committee for Study of Invention. 2004. Invention: Enhancing Inventiveness for Quality of Life, Competitiveness, and Sustainability. Report of the Committee for Study of Invention, sponsored by the Lemelson-MIT Program and the National Science Foundation. Available online at *http://web.mit.edu/invent/n-pressreleases/downloads/report_web.pdf.* Accessed February 4, 2005.

Davidson, C. I., and S. A. Ambrose. 1994. *The New Professor's Handbook: A Guide to Teaching and Research in Engineering and Science.* Bolton, Mass.: Anker.

Downey, G., and J. Lucena. 1998. Engineering Selves: Hiring in to a Contested Field of Engineering Education. Pp. 117–142 in *Cyborgs & Citadels: Anthropological Interventions in Emerging Sciences and Technologies,* G. Downey and J. Dumit, eds. Santa Fe, N.Mex.: School of American Research Press.

Evans, D. L. 2002. In *Visions 2020: Transforming Education and Training Through Advanced Technologies.* Washington, D.C.: Interagency Working Group on Advanced Technology for Education and Training, National Science and Technology Council. Available online at *http://www.visions2020.gov/reports/TechPolicy/2020Visions.pdf.* Accessed July 8, 2005.

Fromm, E. 2002. The Changing Engineering Education Paradigm. Bernard M. Gordon Lecture, National Academy of Engineering, October 6. Available online at *http:// www.nae.edu/NAE/awardscom.nsf/weblinks/LRAO-5EQTF5?OpenDocument.* Accessed July 12, 2005.

Goodman, I. F., C. M. Cunningham, C. Lachapelle, M. Thompson, K. Bittinger, R. T. Brennan, and M. Delci. 2002. Final Report of the Women's Experiences in College Engineering (WECE) Project. Cambridge, Mass.: Goodman Research Group, Inc. Available online at *http://www.grginc.com/WECE_FINAL_REPORT.pdf.* Accessed July 9, 2005.

Hestenes, D., M. Wells, and G. Swackhamer. 1992. Force concept inventory. *The Physics Teacher* 30:141–158.

Knight, D. W., L. E. Carlson, and J. F. Sullivan. 2003. Staying in engineering: Impact of a hands-on, team based, First-Year Projects course on student retention. In *Proceedings of the 2003 American Society for Engineering Education Annual Conference & Exposition.* Washington, D.C.: American Society for Engineering Education. Available online at *http://itll.colorado.edu/ITLL/Templates/ITLInTheMedia/Papers/ASEE%2003% 20Retention%20GEEN%201400%20Proceedings.pdf.* Accessed May 4, 2005.

Massachusetts Department of Education. May 2001. Science and Technology/Engineering Curriculum Framework. Malden, Mass.

May, G. S., and D. E. Chubin. 2003. A retrospective on undergraduate engineering success for underrepresented minority students. *Journal of Engineering Education* 92(1):33.

NAE (National Academy of Engineering). 2004. *The Engineer of 2020: Visions of Engineering in the New Century.* Washington, D.C.: The National Academies Press.

NRC (National Research Council). 1999. *How People Learn: Brain, Mind, Experience, and School.* Washington, D.C.: National Academy Press.

Seymour, E., and Hewitt, N. M. 1997. *Talking About Leaving: Why Undergraduates Leave the Sciences.* Boulder, Colo.: Westview Press.

5

Recommendations

ASPIRATIONS AND ATTRIBUTES OF ENGINEERS OF 2020

Within the context of the changing national and global landscape, the Phase I committee enunciated a set of aspirations for engineers in 2020. These aspirations set the bar high but are believed attainable if a course of action is set to reach them. At their core they call for us to educate technically proficient engineers who are broadly educated, see themselves as global citizens, can be leaders in business and public service, and who are ethically grounded. The committee took the aspirations a step further by setting forth the attributes needed for the graduates of 2020 to reach them. These include such traits as strong analytical skills, creativity, ingenuity, professionalism, and leadership. It is our hope and expectation that the implementation of the recommendations below will allow these aspirations and desired attributes to be met.

REENGINEERING THE ENGINEERING
EDUCATION SYSTEM

Given the changing landscape sketched in the Phase I report, a number of possible implications for engineering education were evident. Supplemented by discussions at the Summit and deliberations by the Phase II committee, these "implications" formed the basis for the recommendations set forth below.

It is evident that the exploding body of science and engineering knowledge cannot be accommodated within the context of the traditional four-year baccalaureate degree. Technical excellence is *the* essential attribute of engineering graduates, but those graduates should also possess team, communication, ethical reasoning, and societal and global contextual analysis skills as well as understand work strategies. Neglecting development in these arenas and learning disciplinary technical subjects to the exclusion of a selection of humanities, economics, political science, language, and/or interdisciplinary technical subjects is not in the best interest of producing engineers able to communicate with the public, able to engage in a global engineering marketplace, or trained to be lifelong learners. Thus, we recommend that

1. The baccalaureate degree should be recognized as the "pre-engineering" degree or bachelor of arts in engineering degree, depending on the course content and reflecting the career aspirations of the student.

Industry and professional societies should recognize and reward the distinction between an entry-level engineer and an engineer who masters an engineering discipline's "body of knowledge" through further formal education or self-study followed by examination. The engineering education establishment must also adopt a broader view of the value of an engineering education to include providing a "liberal" engineering education to those students who wish to use it as a springboard for other career pursuits, such as business, medicine, or law. Adequate depth in a specialized area of engineering cannot be achieved in the baccalaureate degree.

To promote the stature of the profession, engineering schools should create accredited "professional" master's degree programs intended to expand and improve the skills and enhance the ability of an engineer to practice engineering. Thus, as an addendum to Recommendation 1, we recommend that

2. ABET should allow accreditation of engineering programs of the same name at the baccalaureate and graduate levels in the same department to recognize that education through a "professional" master's degree produces an AME, an accredited "master" engineer.

With the increased robustness of information technology and the rapidly expanding number of educational models being developed at engineering campuses, one could conceive of an engineering "program" at institution A that consists, in part, of courses offered online by institutions B and C, and internships at industrial site D. As long as institution A defines its outcome goals, has rigorous metrics for their attainment, and stands behind the "program," one can conceive that such an approach could be accredited. Such a hypothetical model is meant to be illustrative of unconventional approaches that can be explored. A renewed effort to mine the promising approaches that were developed by the coalitions could be a source of inspiration for such efforts. Thus, we recommend that

3. Engineering schools should more vigorously exploit the flexibility inherent in the outcomes-based accreditation approach to experiment with novel models for baccalaureate education. ABET should ensure that evaluators look for innovation and experimentation in the curriculum and not just hold institutions to a strict interpretation of the guidelines as they see them.

Based on the curricular experiments that have been conducted under the National Science Foundation (NSF) Coalitions Program, it is apparent that students who are introduced to engineering design, engineering problem solving, and the concept of engineering as a servant of society early in their undergraduate education are more likely to pursue their engineering programs to completion. The same approach apparently is also more appealing to women and underrepresented minority students who are in such short supply in engineering programs and much more likely to drop out. Treating the freshman year as a "sink or swim" experience and accepting attrition as inevitable is both unfair to students and wasteful of resources and faculty time. Thus, we recommend that

4. Whatever other creative approaches are taken in the four-year engineering curriculum, the essence of engineering—the iterative process of designing, predicting performance, building, and testing—should be taught from the earliest stages of the curriculum, including the first year.

Curricular approaches that engage students in team exercises, in team design courses, and as noted above, in courses that connect engineering design and solutions to real-world problems so that the social relevance of engineering is apparent appear to be successful in retaining students. However, the designs of such approaches and assessment of their effectiveness in terms of how to evaluate individual student performance are still not well rooted in rigorous investigation. Changes in engineering learning experiences involving curricula, pedagogies, and support services should be based on research on learning. Thus, we recommend that

5. The engineering education establishment, for example, the Engineering Deans Council, should endorse research in engineering education as a valued and rewarded activity for engineering faculty as a means to enhance and personalize the connection to undergraduate students, to understand how they learn, and to appreciate the pedagogical approaches that excite them.

At the application end of engineering practice, there is a growing disconnect with engineering education that begs for enlightened industrial engineering leaders and a new generation of faculty able to bridge the gap more effectively. For their part, if engineering faculty, as a group, are to adequately prepare students for practice, then some population within that group must have credible experience in the world of nonacademic practice. This is not a recommendation that all engineering faculty must have "n" years of experience in industry. It is a recommendation that departments need to more closely examine the mix of skills and experiences possessed across their cadre of faculty to determine how best to provide students with the knowledge and experiences essential to engineering practice. The engineering education establishment should strengthen the ties binding engineering education to practice not only through curricular design and provision of co-curricular activities, but through the experiences of engineering faculty in industrial research, product design, and/or production. Thus, we recommend that

6. Colleges and universities should develop new standards for faculty qualifications, appointments, and expectations, for example, to require experience as a practicing engineer, and should create or

adapt development programs to support the professional growth of engineering faculty.

The half-life of cutting-edge technical knowledge today is on the order of a few years, but globalization of the economy is accelerating and the international marketplace for engineering services is dynamic. In such an environment, an engineer is like a small boat in a storm-tossed sea if he or she cannot recognize global trends and lacks the ability, instinct, or desire for continuous learning. In the vein that one can provide the means, if not ensure the ends, we recommend that

7. As well as delivering content, engineering schools must teach engineering students how to learn, and must play a continuing role along with professional organizations in facilitating lifelong learning, perhaps through offering "executive" technical degrees similar to executive MBAs.

Real-world problems are rarely defined along narrow disciplinary lines. Undergraduate students would benefit from at least cursory learning about the interplay between disciplines embodied in such problems. Thus, we recommend that

8. Engineering schools introduce interdisciplinary learning in the undergraduate environment, rather than having it as an exclusive feature of the graduate programs.

It is sometimes said that, when a technical effort goes poorly, valuable knowledge from that failure is lost, the innocent are sacrificed, and the guilty are promoted. This dooms future engineers to make the same mistakes. The management of knowledge is somewhat better in the case of successes, but it is questionable whether the real elements of success are identified separate of the marketing "spin" for the product or service. In this case, following the "same" path to success may be an illusion. In the interest of promoting success and avoiding failure, we recommend that

9. Engineering educators should explore the development of case studies of engineering successes and failures and the appropriate

use of a case-studies approach in undergraduate and graduate curricula.

Approximately 40 percent of baccalaureate graduate engineers have had some community college experience along the way. Community colleges provide a vital pathway for an engineering education for lower income students, from both majority and underrepresented groups. Facilitating articulation between two-year and four-year engineering programs is a critical factor in ensuring that the pool of potential engineering students from two-year institutions has a fair opportunity to complete a four-year degree. Ironically, the greater flexibility provided to four-year schools by the ABET Engineering Criteria 2000 makes the dovetailing of curricula more difficult. Thus, we recommend that

10. Four-year engineering schools must accept it as their responsibility to work with their local community colleges to ensure effective articulation, as seamless as possible, with their two-year programs.

Graduate students from all over the world have flocked to the United States for years to take advantage of the excellent graduate education available. U.S. universities must recognize that there is rapidly increasing competition for these international Ph.D. students that will likely persist even if post-9/11 immigration challenges and restrictions subside. They must posture themselves to compete for foreign graduate students, who have typically represented half the "life blood" of engineering departments. At the same time, however, they cannot afford to neglect domestic students. Indeed, improvements in engineering education that energize the undergraduate experience may encourage more domestic students to pursue advanced degrees. Thus, we recommend that

11. U.S. engineering schools must develop programs to encourage/ reward domestic engineering students to aspire to the M.S. and/or Ph.D. degree.

To recruit the most highly qualified, best-prepared students from the nation's secondary school system, colleges, universities, and community colleges should play a prominent role in ensuring that all Americans have the opportunity to pursue an engineering education, if they so choose. There are many local efforts in progress to help secondary school students understand the nature of engineering and some, such as Project Lead the Way and the Infinity Project, which are active in multiple states. Efforts to share successful practices from these programs and propagate them even further are essential. Thus, we recommend that

12. Engineering schools should lend their energies to a national effort to improve math, science, and engineering education at the K-12 level.

It is in the enlightened self-interest of engineering schools to help the public understand what engineers do and the role that engineering plays in ensuring their quality of life. Moreover, a country weak in technological literacy will have increasing difficulty competing in the technology-driven global economy of the twenty-first century. Thus, we recommend that

13. The engineering education establishment should participate in a coordinated national effort to promote public understanding of engineering and technology literacy of the public.

As indicated in a paper by Busch-Vishniac and Jarosz, provided to the Summit participants, there appears to be an unlimited number of different engineering curricula structures and the attendant engineering education schemes they imply offered by the multitude of engineering programs across the country (2004). While engineering faculty, as experts in the domain, might understand and appreciate the different possible approaches, it is highly unlikely that a high school junior or senior, his or her guidance counselor, or parents could understand the alternatives and deduce which scheme and which school might be most suitable for enrollment. In the spirit that the engineering community must "sell" the value and excitement of an engineering education, the community must make every effort to help interested students make an informed choice. The American Society of Engineering Education (ASEE) has an excellent website (*http://www.asee.org/about/publications/ profiles/index.cfm#Online_Profiles*) containing statistical profiles of undergraduate engineering programs, but we believe that it would also be informative to collect information from the point of view of the student, for example, about program philosophy—engineering up front, availability of team design activities, etc., and about student outcomes in terms of retention, years to degree completion and securing jobs at graduation.

14. NSF should collect and/or fund collection, perhaps through ASEE or the Engineering Workforce Commission, of comprehensive data by engineering department/school on program philosophy and student outcomes such as, but not exclusively, student retention rates by gender and ethnicity, common reasons why students leave, where they go, percent of entering freshman that graduate, time to degree, and information on jobs and admission to graduate school.

REFERENCE

Busch-Vishniac, I., and J. Jarosz. 2004. Can diversity in the undergraduate engineering population be enhanced through curricular change? *Journal of Women in Science and Technology* 10(3).

Appendix A

The reports included here were prepared as background information for the consideration of Summit attendees prior to the meeting. They represent the opinions of the authors and are not necessarily endorsed by the Engineer of 2020 Phase II Committee. The committee wishes to express its appreciation for the efforts of the authors in preparing these reports.

A Brief Summary of Cooperative Education: History, Philosophy, and Current Status

Thomas M. Akins
Georgia Institute of Technology

In a recent survey conducted by MonsterTRAK of college graduates in 2004, 74 percent thought relevant work experience was the most important factor in securing employment, and 52 percent of employers agreed. However, 41 percent of the students had gotten *no* relevant experience during their undergraduate careers. For those students, finding a job and deciding on a career choice can be much more difficult than for those who have experience. Cooperative education, a time-tested method of enhancing learning, gives students such experience and enables them to achieve much more than their counterparts who are educated in the traditional way.

DEFINITION/PHILOSOPHY

Cooperative education primarily involves sequential training in both theory and practice; theoretical and practical training are coordinated in a progressive educational program. For both school and student, studies become "applied subjects" because theory (studies) is realized through practical application (work). With feedback from employers on student performance, cooperative education is also a great vehicle for outcome-based assessment of the undergraduate curriculum. From the employer's point of view, the two most important elements in cooperative education are (1) the selection of workers and (2) an enlightened interest on the part of students in the work.

For the purposes of this paper, I use a traditional definition of a cooperative education program adapted from the "The Cooperative System—a Manifesto," an article by Clement Freund in the *Journal of Engineering Education* in October 1946.

A cooperative education program shall be one:

- in which curricula lead to the bachelor's, master's or doctoral degree
- that requires or permits all or some students to alternate periods of attendance at college with periods of employment in business/industry during a portion or all of one or more curricula
- in which such employment is constituted as a regular, continuing, and essential element in the educational process
- that requires such employment to be related to some phase of the branch or field of study in which the student is engaged
- that expects such employment to be diverse so that students have a wide range of experience
- that expects such employment to have work assignments with increasing levels of responsibility on successive work terms
- that specifies as requirements for a degree a minimum number of hours of employment and a minimum standard of performance in such employment

SPECIFIC GOALS OF COOPERATIVE EDUCATION

Freund also detailed five specific aims of cooperative education that are still embraced today:

1. To impart first-hand and actual knowledge of and experience with the execution in industry/government of engineering designs, business principles, projects, and developments in all career fields.
2. To impart understanding of and familiarity with the problems and viewpoints of working men and women.
3. To assist students, by direct and personal experience in industry, in testing their aptitudes for their chosen careers.
4. To enable students to adjust to employment by a gradual transition from academic pursuits to the requirements and conditions of the world of work.

5. To train and otherwise prepare students especially and directly for higher level administrative and operating functions.

HISTORY

In the 1890s, many colleges realized the need for better integration of theory and practice. At Worcester Polytechnic Institute, regular shop courses began operating a commercial shop and offering articles for sale. Students worked in the shop for foremen/instructors. The school also advised students to work in industry for 15 months between their junior and senior years. All of this was to be supplanted by an idea that took shape in the mind of Herman Schneider, a civil engineering graduate of Lehigh University who had worked his way through school.

Schneider believed that his work experience had given him an advantage upon graduation. He researched the records of other Lehigh graduates and found that most of those who had shown marked ability in engineering during the early years after graduation had combined industry practice with education through part-time jobs, summer jobs, or simply by dropping out of school to work periodically. Schneider concluded that the educational values of working exceeded the monetary gains.

When he joined the faculty of the University of Cincinnati in 1903 (as assistant professor of civil engineering), he envisioned a new kind of institution that would blend theory and practice so students could provide industry with the services for which they were being prepared. In September 1906, the first cooperative education program began with 12 students in mechanical engineering, 12 in electrical engineering, and 3 in chemical engineering. In the beginning, they alternated between school and work weekly, then every two weeks, then monthly, then quarterly.

Other schools soon followed suit: Northeastern University in 1909, University of Pittsburgh in 1910 (although the program was discontinued for many years and reestablished in 1987), University of Detroit in 1911, and Georgia Tech in 1912. In the early years, cooperative education programs experienced various external and internal problems. External problems included: resistance among employers; recessions/depressions; wars; and resistance among labor unions. Internal problems at schools included: hesitant faculty; scheduling and alternating patterns; mandatory versus optional programs; and funding. Most of the external problems are beyond institutional control, of course. But many schools continue to wrestle with internal problems. As Herman Schneider stated in a speech in 1929, "There are no two cooperative courses the same, and different tactics have to be used in different places. I hope there will never be two programs the same."

As the number of programs grew, it became apparent that educational professionals could benefit from sharing ideas and concerns. In 1926, the Association of Cooperative Colleges was established; it later became the Cooperative Education Division of what is now the American Society for Engineering Education. The National Commission for Cooperative Education was begun in 1962, and the Cooperative Education Association was formed in 1963. The World Association of Cooperative Education started in 1979, and there are numerous state and regional associations across the United States. Through these organizations, cooperative education programs have been able to present a united front on many issues, particularly in the area of funding for co-op programs on campuses.

The federal government has been instrumental in providing seed money. In 1970, Title IV-D provided a total of more than $1.5 million. Title VIII replaced this in 1977, and by the late 1980s total grants averaged about $15 million per year. By 1989, there were more than 1,000 cooperative programs in the United States with approximately 250,000 students. Later in this paper, I review the current status of co-op programs. However, I want to turn now to a brief summary of the benefits of the cooperative education model.

BENEFITS OF COOPERATIVE EDUCATION

The *Directory of College Cooperative Education Programs*, put out by the American Council on Education, includes lists of advantages of cooperative education to students, employers, schools, and society as a whole (Hutcheson, 1966). The benefits are summarized below (in no particular order):

Advantages to students
- enhances classroom learning through integration of theory and practice
- confirms or redirects career decision making

- helps defray the costs of postsecondary education through wages earned
- expands after-graduation job opportunities
- teaches "soft skills," such as communications, working on multidisciplinary teams, career assessment, resume writing, and interviewing
- encourages traditionally non-college-bound students to pursue postsecondary education

Advantages to employers
- provides a pool of well prepared employees
- provides on-the-job performance as a basis for permanent hiring decisions
- enhances relations between businesses and colleges
- improves access to permanent employment for students from disadvantaged (underrepresented) groups
- makes recruitment and training more cost effective
- increases retention rates among permanent employees
- provides a means of technology (knowledge) transfer

Advantages to postsecondary institutions
- expands the range of educational opportunities by integrating workplace learning into the academic program
- builds positive relationships between schools and industry
- enables the enrollment and education of more students without the expansion of physical facilities, especially in an alternating program in which a large number of students are at work each term
- provides a means of technology (knowledge) transfer

Advantages to society
- increases the effectiveness and relevance of education by relating classroom study to the world of work
- promotes respect for work
- addresses national concerns about the preparation of the future workforce for competition in a global economy
- does not add costs to taxpayers because cooperative education returns sizable tax revenues from student earnings

CURRENT STATUS

In 1989, there were more than 1,000 cooperative education programs of various kinds in postsecondary institutions throughout the United States; approximately 250,000 students were enrolled in these programs. At the same time, 34,089 students were enrolled in engineering and engineering technology cooperative programs at 104 schools. As Title VIII funding disappeared, however, many schools could no longer provide financial support for these programs, and, consequently, a large number of them were dissolved. The latest figures below show the number of undergraduate students participating in cooperative programs in engineering and engineering technology (Mathews, 1998, 2000, 2002, 2004):

- 1998, 142 schools, 38,734 students
- 2000, 118 schools, 31,716 students
- 2002, 121 schools, 36,718 students
- 2004, 99 schools, 34,136 students

One might ask why the number of programs, and particularly the number of students, has not increased over the years. Here are some possible answers based on conjecture and anecdotal information:

- Students are opting for more internships, rather than making commitments to cooperative programs.
- More financial aid is available now than ever before, which eliminates the monetary incentive for participating in a co-op program.
- Because of the "blue-collar" connotation of cooperative programs, faculty and administration at many institutions have not fully embraced the idea.
- Some misconceptions and "myths" about cooperative education have discouraged participation (e.g., that it takes longer to graduate; that co-op students cannot participate in campus activities or study abroad, etc.).

Recent research at Georgia Tech has shown that rising family income levels of entering students and the availability of other options, such as undergraduate research and internships, have been major factors in the declining enrollment in cooperative education at that institution. Interestingly, students who participate in cooperative programs at Georgia Tech actually do take about six months longer to graduate, but they enroll in fewer school terms to do so, thus saving tuition money in the long run. Many of these students also participate in study abroad programs and undergraduate research, which dispels some widely held misconceptions.

ACCREDITATION DATA

I would be remiss if I did not mention the value of co-op programs to the accreditation of engineering programs. Recently, accrediting organizations, including the Accreditation Board for Engineering and Technology (ABET), have moved toward outcomes-based assessments of programs. Engineering Criteria 2000, which was begun by ABET several years ago, includes students' ability to perform certain functions, such as working on multidisciplinary teams, applying engineering knowledge, and so forth. Consequently, engineering deans and provosts at many institutions have discovered the value of data collected by their co-op programs. In fact, information gathered from employers' evaluations of co-op students' performance has been invaluable in determining, from a third-party source, if the education received on campus is not only thorough, but also relevant enough to prepare individuals for the transition from "student" to professional.

CONCLUSION

In the future, there will be many models for engineering education. However, the concept of cooperative education still makes good fiscal sense, good pedagogical sense, and good career sense. Cooperative education opens a myriad of possibilities for anyone pursuing a formal education at the postsecondary level. Although its form may change from one generation to the next, there is no substitute for blending practical application with theory learned in the classroom, and there is no better laboratory than the real world. Future leaders of technology must have experience outside the classroom to function effectively.

REFERENCES

Freund, C.J. 1946. The co-operative system: a manifesto. Journal of Engineering Education 37(2): 117–120.

Hutcheson, P., ed. 1996. Directory of College Cooperative Programs. Washington, D.C.: American Council on Education.

Mathews, J.M., ed. 1998. Directory of Engineering and Engineering Technology Co-op Programs. Mississippi State, Miss.: Cooperative Education Division of the American Society for Engineering Education.

Mathews, J.M., ed. 2000. Directory of Engineering and Engineering Technology Co-op Programs. Mississippi State, Miss.: Cooperative Education Division of the American Society for Engineering Education.

Mathews, J.M., ed. 2002. Directory of Engineering and Engineering Technology Co-op Programs. Mississippi State, Miss.: Cooperative Education Division of the American Society for Engineering Education.

Mathews, J.M., ed. 2004. Directory of Engineering and Engineering Technology Co-op Programs. Mississippi State, Miss.: Cooperative Education Division of the American Society for Engineering Education.

MonsterTRAK. 2004. College Graduation Survey. Maynard, Mass.: Monster. Available online at *http://www.monster.com*.

Schneider, H. 1929. Remarks delivered at the 4th Annual Conference of the Association of Cooperative Colleges, June 21, 1929, Columbus, Ohio. Washington, D.C.: American Society for Engineering Education.

Information Technology in Support of Engineering Education: Lessons from the Greenfield Coalition

Donald R. Falkenburg
Greenfield Coalition
Wayne State University

Many studies have focused on the impact of information technology (IT). To frame the discussion in this paper, I call your attention to two quotes from a section called Technology Futures in *Preparing for the Revolution: Information Technology and the Future of the Research University* published by the National Academies Press (NRC, 2002).

From the average user's point of view, the exponential rate dictated by Moore's Law will drive increases of 100 to 1,000 in computing speed, storage capacity, and bandwidth every decade. At that pace, today's $1,000-notebook computer will, by the year 2020, have a computing speed of 1 million gigahertz, a memory of thousands of terabytes, and linkages to networks at data transmission speeds of gigabits per second.

. . . [T]he world of the user could be marked by increasing technological sophistication. With virtual reality, individuals may routinely communicate with one another through simulated environments, or "telepresence," perhaps delegating their own digital representations—"software agents," or tools that collect, organize, relate, and summarize knowledge on behalf of their human masters— to interact in a virtual world with those of their colleagues. As communications technology increases in power by 100 fold (or more) each decade, such digitally mediated human interactions could take place with essentially any degree of fidelity desired.

In a National Academy of Engineering workshop, Information Technology (IT)-Based Educational Materials, this future vision was translated into the framework of teaching and learning. In the workshop report, the current state of the use of IT in support of learning was described (NAE, 2003):

> Many STEM [science, technology, engineering, and mathematics] educational programs and institutions have been involved in projects to improve teaching and learning through the application of IT. The resulting IT-based learning materials have proven to be adaptable and dynamic, and in many cases they have enhanced the educational process. A growing number of people are involved in the development of IT-based educational materials. The landscape of STEM education is now dotted with islands of innovation—isolated areas where IT-based materials are being used effectively. However, not all innovations have led to more effective learning because these materials are often used by limited numbers of users. Thus, opportunities for synergy, discourse, and exchange—steps that often lead to improvements in next-generation products—have also been limited. Impediments to realizing a desirable environment for IT-based educational materials are complex. . . . [T]echnology and tools, infrastructure, content and pedagogy, and human, cultural, and organizational issues . . . are inextricably intertwined.

Based on the workshop discussions, the participants developed a vision of an IT-transformed educational environment summarized in three broad categories: technology and tools infrastructure; content and pedagogy; and human, cultural, and organizational frameworks. The discussions were summarized in the following vision of the future (NAE, 2003):

> A robust suite of modular, IT-based resources supports a dynamic, distributed, and flexible learning environment. Built on open system architectures and machine-understandable semantic models, these resources are interoperable, sharable, easy to use, easy to modify, and widely disseminated; they underpin a vibrant teaching and learning community and enable a sustainable ecology for continuous improvements in educational practice. A rich array of technologies and

approaches form the scaffolding for further modifications to the learning environment, enabling the optimization of educational practices for their effectiveness rather than for simple efficiency. The elements that support the learning environment integrate advanced knowledge about technology, people, processes, and organizations.

The report also included the following descriptions of the future:

In the world of IT-transformed education, advanced learning objects are the building blocks of IT-enabled educational materials. Advanced learning objects will be developed based on community-defined requirements for a services-based architecture that supports varying levels of interoperability and emphasizes operational communication and data exchange.

STEM educational practices will have a learner-centric orientation and will reflect advanced, evidence-based knowledge on learning and cognition.

IT-based teaching and learning practices will be generated by an active community of authors and users who create, share, and modify IT-enabled educational materials. This community will embrace a scholarship of teaching and learning and will have a continuing goal of advancing learning.

The dissemination of IT-enabled teaching and learning resources will be supported by a novel legal framework (e.g., open licenses and attribution systems) that promotes creation and sharing, while maintaining incentives for authors (including individuals, teams, and institutions) to create and distribute or assemble and reuse high-quality learning materials.

In the remainder of this paper, I briefly describe the efforts of the Greenfield Coalition to move toward this IT-enhanced learning future.

INFORMATION TECHNOLOGY IN
SUPPORT OF PEDAGOGY

One of the lessons learned at the Greenfield Coalition was that, even though IT can open new avenues to enhance learning, technology is not a silver bullet that can promote learning by itself. We posed the following question: What do we want to accomplish by using IT to support the learning process? The answer reflects the Greenfield Coalition's values and beliefs about learning:

- Learning is a responsibility shared by learner and teacher.
- Faculty plays a key role in guiding students in the learning process.
- Learning is made real if it is integrated with real-world experience.
- Learners must prepare to engage in classroom experiences.
- Learning is a social process that requires interaction with mentors and peers.
- By actively participating in learning, students can reach a deeper understanding and enhance their skills.

IT must be leveraged not for its own sake, but in support of a vision of the transformed classroom. There are many issues we might consider, but I illustrate two here.

Case Studies: Engaging Learners in Decision Making Framed in Real-World Environments

---

In the future, improved hardware and software will enhance simulated virtual environments in which learners can become immersed in the problem-solving and decision making experience.

Case studies have revolutionized teaching in the business and medical communities. The case-study methodology is a framework for embedding learning in an environment as close to the real world as possible, challenging learners to explore resources, make assumptions, and construct solutions. Case studies are also ideal for illustrating complex concepts, which are especially common in engineering. Horton (2000) suggests that case studies are an excellent way for learners to practice judgment skills necessary in real-life situations, which are not as simple as textbook problems. Stimulating critical thinking through case studies is a recommended instructional strategy (Bonk and Reynolds, 1997).

In the current educational environment, computer-based resources allow learners to access real data and participate in case-based learning (Falkenburg and Schuch Miller, 2003). For example, students can explore a real factory of a tier-1 auto supplier, with access to process plans, production data, scrap reports, and interviews with key personnel. Figure 1 displays the web interface for a case developed by the Greenfield Coalition, which targets a boring operation used in the manufacture of a pulley. In the future, with improved hardware and software, learners will be able to immerse themselves in the problem-solving and decision-making experience. Instead of "canned" interviews, the learner and intelligent computer systems will provide responses to learner inquiries.

Case studies can also be used to introduce students to the complex interactions among technology, business, and ethics. The Laboratory for Innovative Technology in Engineering Education at Auburn University has produced a number of case studies. One of these describes a turbine-generator unit in a power plant that vibrates heavily enough to shake the building. Two engineers recommend different solutions, and the plant manager must make a decision that could cost the company millions of dollars (Raju and Sankar, 2000).

Simulation: Improving Understanding and Decision Making

Many of us already feel comfortable teaching computer simulation to enhance problem-solving skills. The problem is that we most frequently focus on the development of computer models to represent an engineering component or system, and we frequently forget to talk about the reason we build models—to improve students' ability to make engineering decisions.

The future will bring improved methods of simulating real-world systems. Those simulations will be easier to construct and encapsulate very real views. Simulation technology should be used early in the career of the student engineer, not to teach modeling per se, but to enhance the student's ability to make engineering decisions.

In Manufacturing Systems, a sophomore-level Greenfield Coalition course developed by Professor Emory Zimmers at Lehigh University, learners are introduced to Colebee Time Management Incorporated, a firm that has determined that rapid order fulfillment is one of their competitive advantages. As they move toward producing more

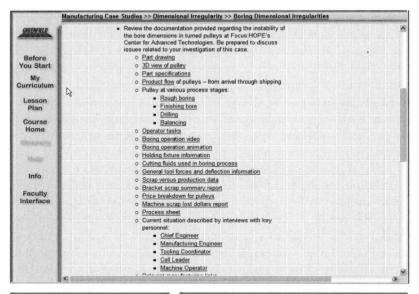

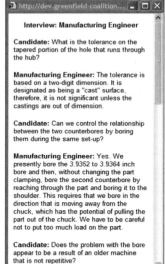

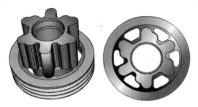

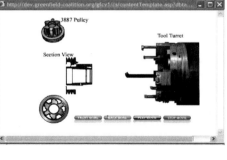

FIGURE 1 Computer resources supporting a Greenfield Coalition case study.

customized planners and calendars, they find they need more analysis of the printing cell, because more varieties of products and smaller batch sizes have slowed printing.

When a new printing job arrives, it must wait until the current group of jobs is completed. When all of the jobs in the current group are finished, the new jobs are lined up in a specific order. The student's task is to improve the operational efficiency of the printing cell by minimizing the so-called "make-span" (the time it takes to complete the entire group of parts ready to proceed into the process). A simulation model of a printing cell is provided to help students predict operational improvements to the system (see Figure 2). The students are told that make-span should be their primary focus, but they may want to also pay attention to the queue sizes and the average time jobs remain in the printing area. They are told that they can manage three key parameters: (1) the number of work centers; (2) the number of hours per shift; and (3) the number of shifts per week.

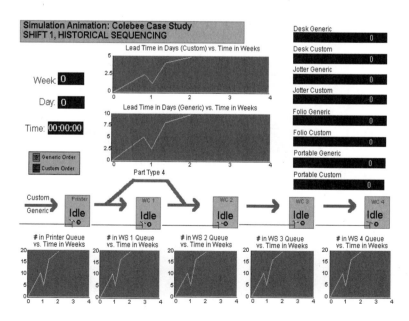

FIGURE 2 Simulation animation for the Colebee case study.

The learners are asked the following key questions:

- What strategy did you use to select the parameters to improve operational efficiency?
- If you could modify the simulation model to allow more parameters to be changed, which parameters would you choose to add? Explain your answer.
- Which combination of parameters optimized the manufacturing plant's operations? Explain your answer.

This case is not about building a computer model. It is about making engineering decisions. In the future, methods of simulating real-world systems will certainly improve. Simulations will be easier to construct and will encapsulate very real views. These improvements should be introduced early in the careers of student engineers, not to teach modeling per se, but to improve their ability to make engineering decisions.

LEARNING OBJECTS

The Greenfield learning object model (LOM, Figure 3) recognizes a hierarchy of learning objects (Falkenburg et al., 2003). At the base of

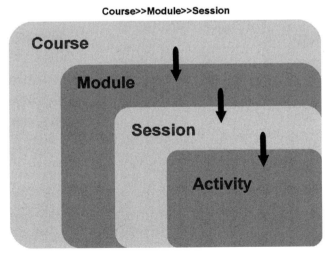

FIGURE 3 Greenfield Learning Object Model.

the model are learning activities focused on the process of learning. Learning activities are dynamically configured into sessions, modules, and courses. In Greenfield parlance, "activities" include discussions, computer-based animations and simulations, mini-lectures, cooperative problem-solving exercises, and so forth—in other words, activities that address the "action" of learning. "Sessions" are groups of activities. Greenfield does not define a time frame for sessions. They are simply convenient groupings of activities. "Modules" are concept-frame packages of learning. A module includes one or more sessions.

The Greenfield course Engineering Economics, for example, includes Depreciation Accounting (a module), which includes Depreciation Methodologies and Income Tax Impact (sessions). Income Tax Impact Consequences is an interactive e-learning activity in the Income Tax Impact session.

We had an important reason for developing this hierarchical structure, namely, that most faculty members want to structure their own courses. Although teachers may be interested in borrowing some "neat" learning activities, they want to package learning in their own unique ways. Thus, each learning activity is an individual entity. Using a methodology that is becoming more common each day, we define the structure of the learning activity, describe its content using XML, and display the activity on a web page using XSL templates (Figure 4).

Links up the hierarchy are constructed differently. If a course is shared, the uplinks are displayed on a tool bar. The content of the tool bar is a property of the assembled course and depends upon the position of the learner in the hierarchy. For a user currently accessing an activity, the tool bar would look as depicted in Figure 3. Courses contain links to modules that are included in their content. If the user is at the session level, the tool bar would show Course>>Module. A module contains links to sessions, are a part of the module content.

Objectives are included in the definition of learning objects. Objectives are defined at the course level (terminal objectives) and at the module and session levels (enabling objectives—objectives that support the

FIGURE 4 Implementing the Greenfield LOM structure.

terminal objectives of a course). Because objectives are included in the object structure of a course, it is a straightforward process to produce a tree of learning objectives.

There are two additional levels in the Greenfield object structure—the program and knowledge areas. A "knowledge area" is a group of courses that share certain instructional objectives and outcomes. For example, in a program that focuses on manufacturing engineering, there are typically courses that focus on manufacturing systems and courses that focus on manufacturing processes. By defining programs in this way, we can provide a tree of objectives for an entire program. By treating prerequisite knowledge as a "child object" of a course, for example, we can better manage requirements for a full curriculum. Meta-tags embedded at each level of the hierarchy define content, special technology support requirements, etc.

Authorship and intellectual property rights are embedded in the objects. Thus, a document with multiple authors can be created by referencing different objects. Data about use restrictions and ownership are drawn from the database and displayed in the composite document.

CHANGING OUR CULTURE

Technology provides one platform for reforming our educational processes, but technology cannot make a difference unless people and organizations change and adapt. The Greenfield Coalition is in the final phase of a research study of the factors that enhance, and the factors that impede, the diffusion of learning technologies. Each classroom is an arena in which the culture of learners and the culture of teachers must negotiate their beliefs, values, and behaviors. Changes in educational process are not simply a matter of adopting IT. IT must also lead to changes in our approaches to learning enabled by that technology. Does IT give us a better means of enhancing modern approaches to learning (Bloom, 1956; Gagne, 1985; Filipczak, 1996), or does it merely divert future engineers from a deeper understanding and better decision making?

THE GREENFIELD COALITION AND FOCUS: HOPE

The Greenfield Coalition and Focus: HOPE is a coalition of five universities, three university affiliates, six manufacturing companies, the

Society of Manufacturing Engineers, and Focus: HOPE. The impetus for the Greenfield Coalition project was a sense that most academic studies in manufacturing engineering did not include real manufacturing experiences (Falkenburg and Harkin, 2002). The idea for the coalition was initiated by Focus: HOPE, a human and civil rights organization in Detroit, Michigan.

Focus: HOPE supports a network of programs that support its educational objectives. Founded in 1968 after the urban riots in Detroit, Focus: HOPE "pledges intelligent and practical action to overcome racism, poverty and injustice"—to make a difference in the city and suburbs. The organization began by providing food for needy people who were undernourished (women with children and then senior citizens) but quickly added programs to give inner-city youth an opportunity to acquire the knowledge they need to take advantage of highly skilled, good-paying jobs.

Today, an individual may enroll in First Step or Fast Track, four- and seven-week programs that use computer-based learning to build fundamental skills in mathematics and English. Students who graduate from Fast Track have skills certified at the ninth-grade and tenth-grade levels in reading and math, the prerequisite skills for entering the Machinist Training Institute (MTI). MTI is a 31-week program in which students earn certification in the operation of material-processing equipment (machining), metrology, computer-aided design, computer numerical control, and associated math, computer, and communication skills.

Greenfield provides an opportunity for graduates of MTI to cap their practical experience with courses that could lead to advanced university degrees. Students who qualify after completing MTI's basic machining program can enter a 24-week preengineering program. After a series of diagnostic tests and interviews, they can then become candidates in the Center for Advanced Technologies—Focus: HOPE's manufacturing facility, a not-for-profit entity and a first-tier supplier of manufactured components and systems to Ford, General Motors, DaimlerChrysler, Detroit Diesel, and the U.S. Department of Defense. Candidates are employed by Focus: HOPE and work in a broad range of manufacturing, production, and support activities. This employment not only provides financial support, but, more important, it provides a real-world laboratory that supports learning.

The partners of the Greenfield Coalition saw Focus: HOPE as an

FIGURE 5 Focus: HOPE candidates working in the Center for Advanced Technologies.

opportunity to support a new approach to manufacturing education in which real-world manufacturing applications would drive learning, rather than the more traditional academic approach of theory looking for an application. A key tenet of the Greenfield Coalition's proposal to the National Science Foundation was the integration of production experiences with the work activities of the candidates at the Focus: HOPE Center for Advanced Technologies (see Figure 5).

The framers of the Greenfield Coalition proposal envisaged an educational experience in which candidates would work and study in the same facility. They would experience the functional operations involved in production, and they would be exposed to flexible manufacturing system architectures, manufacturing systems design, and process and quality control. Candidates would rotate through positions in production and manufacturing engineering and learn through their experiences. At the same time, they would be guided by a combination of mentors/teachers, including functional supervisors in the Center for Advanced Technologies, vendor trainers, faculty from coalition universities, and industry experts. Learning would be modular and would provide fundamental skills and understanding to support a progression of work experiences. Thus, the work environment and the learning experience would be mutually supportive. The ultimate goal would be to produce a new breed of engineer who has not only a theoretical under-standing of manufacturing, but also practical, hands-on experience.

Acknowledgments

The Greenfield Coalition is partly supported by Grant EEC-9630951 under the Engineering Education Coalitions Program at the National Science Foundation. Focus: HOPE, the coalition's industry and academic partner, has contributed valuable resources to support the development of the Greenfield Coalition.

REFERENCES

Bloom, B. 1956. Taxonomy of Educational Objectives: The Classification of Education Goals. Handbook I, Cognitive Domain. New York: John Wiley and Sons.

Bonk, C.J., and T.H. Reynolds, 1997. Learner-centered web instruction for higher-order thinking, teamwork, and apprenticeship. In B.H. Khan (Ed.), Web-Based Instruction (pp. 167-178). Englewood Cliffs, N.J.: Educational Technology Publications.

Falkenburg, D.R., and T. Harkin 2002. Real-World Experience in Learning in Manufactur-ing Education Proceedings of the 2002 American Society for Engineering Education Annual Conference and Exposition. Montreal, Quebec, Canada: American Society for Engineering Education. Available online at *http://asee.org/acPapers/code/getPaper.cfm?paperID=5444&pdf=2002-983_Final.pdf.*

Falkenburg, D.R., and D. Schuch Miller. 2003. Strategies for Creating Web-Based Engineer-ing Case Studies. Proceedings of the 2003 International Conference on Engineering Education (ICEE). Valencia, Spain: International Network for Engineering Education and Research. Available online at *http://www.ineer.org/events/icee2003/proceedings/pdf/4478.pdf.*

Falkenburg, D.R., A. Knowlton, and M.J. Cartright. 2003. Creating Sharable Learning Ac-tivities: Examples from a Manufacturing Engineering Curriculum. Proceedings of the 2003 American Society for Engineering Education Annual Conference and Exposition. Nashville, Tenn.: American Society for Engineering Education. Available online at *http://asee.org/acPapers/code/getPaper.cfm?paperID=5608&pdf=2003-1563_Final.pdf.*

Filipczak, B. 1996. Engaged!: The nature of computer interactivity. Training 33(11):52–58.

Gagne, R. 1985. The Conditions of Learning, 4th ed. New York: Holt, Rinehart and Winston.

Horton, W. 2000. Designing Web-Based Training. New York: John Wiley and Sons.

NAE (National Academy of Engineering). 2003. Information Technology (IT)-Based Edu-cational Materials: Workshop Report with Recommendations. Washington, D.C.: Na-tional Academies Press. Available online at *http://books.nap.edu/catalog/10768.html.*

NRC (National Research Council). 2002. Preparing for the Revolution: Information Tech-nology and the Future of the Research University. Washington, D.C.: National Acad-emies Press. Available online at *http://books.nap.edu/catalog/10545.html.*

Raju, P.K., and C.S. Sankar. 2000. Della Steam Plant Case Study: Should the Turbine Be Shut Off? Anderson, S.C.: Tavenner Publishers.

The Engineering Education Coalitions Program

Jeffrey Froyd
Texas A&M University

EXECUTIVE SUMMARY

The National Science Foundation (NSF) supported six engineering-education coalitions (EECs) with the goal of catalyzing systemic reform in engineering education (i.e., changes throughout the system, especially among faculty members, the most important component of the system). The most productive innovations intentionally or unintentionally provoked faculty members into reflecting on and modifying their ideas about learning and teaching. For example, faculty members who participated in interdisciplinary, integrated curricular activities were involved in mutually supportive, thoughtful discussions with their peers about learning, assessment, and teaching. Another project involved the construction of multidisciplinary design projects that exposed faculty members to multiple disciplinary perspectives on the engineering design process. Faculty members also participated in workshops where they were encouraged to consider and apply pedagogical options and alternative learning environments (e.g., active/cooperative learning, problem-based learning, etc.). In another exercise, faculty members were involved in the development of instruments and methodologies to assess students' conceptual understanding of engineering science. All of these activities encouraged faculty members to reflect and reevaluate their approaches to learning and teaching.

The most productive EEC projects led to the development of resources that were intended to make it easier for others to explore innovative approaches. For example, interactive workshops were focused on modeling pedagogical innovations being tried and advocated in the EECs, assessment instruments and methods were developed for assessing student learning, websites provided widespread access to publications and other resources created as a result of EEC activities, and summary documents were produced synthesizing research and innovation in engineering education both as part of the EECs and from other sources.

However, faculty and institutions that had not been directly involved in the EECs showed little interest in adopting these innovations, even when assessment data demonstrated that they led to measurable improvements in retention and/or student learning. Thus, it was clear that catalyzing systemic reform would require more than model programs and approaches that could be adapted by faculty members anywhere. It would require "out-of-the-box" thinking and the active participation of educators in conversations about learning, assessment, and teaching before adoption could be expected.

INTRODUCTION

NSF developed the EEC Program to stimulate the development of models of bold, innovative systemic reforms in undergraduate engineering education. Through the EEC Program, groups of universities and colleges with different characteristics formed coalitions for the purpose of becoming agents of change in the engineering education community. Goals for systemic reform included increasing the retention of students, especially students from underrepresented groups, such as white women and minorities; and improving introductory experiences in engineering through active, experiential learning, such as artifact dissection, and multidisciplinary capstone design experiences. Reforms developed by EECs have reinvigorated undergraduate engineering curricula at institutions throughout the coalitions and beyond and are turning out graduates who are better prepared to meet the challenges of a constantly changing global workforce. At the same time, EEC participating schools (listed in Table 1) have increased diversity, improved student retention, and increased graduation rates.

TABLE 1 Participating Institutions and Contributions of Engineering Education Coalitions

Coalition	Participating Institutions	Major Contributions
Engineering Coalition of Schools for Excellence in Education and Leadership (ECSEL) 1990–2001	City College of the City University of New York Howard University Massachusetts Institute of Technology Morgan State University Pennsylvania State University University of Maryland University of Washington	First-year engineering design courses Assessments of innovative pedagogical approaches
Synthesis (http://www.synthesis.org) 1990–2001	California Polytechnic State University at San Luis Obispo Cornell University Hampton University Iowa State University Southern University Stanford University Tuskegee University University of California at Berkeley	Artifact dissection NEEDS (National Engineering Education Delivery System)
Southeastern University and College Coalition for Engineering Education (SUCCEED) (http://www.succeednow.org) 1992–2003	Clemson University Florida A&M University—Florida State University Georgia Institute of Technology North Carolina Agricultural and Technical State University North Carolina State University University of North Carolina Charlotte	Multidisciplinary capstone design courses SUCCEED longitudinal student database

Coalition	Institutions	Focus
Gateway (*http://www.gatewaycoalition.org*) 1992–2003	University of Florida Virginia Polytechnic Institute and State University Columbia University Cooper Union Drexel University New Jersey Institute of Technology Ohio State University Polytechnic University University of South Carolina	First-year engineering curricula Multimedia modules
Foundation (*http://www.foundationcoalition.org*) 1993–2004	Arizona State University Maricopa Community College District Rose-Hulman Institute of Technology Texas A&M University Texas A&M University Kingsville Texas Women's University University of Alabama University of Massachusetts Dartmouth University of Wisconsin Madison	First two years of engineering curricula Engineering science concept inventory assessment instruments
Greenfield (*http://www.greenfield-coalition.org*) 1994–2005	Lawrence Technological University Lehigh University Michigan State University University of Detroit Mercy Wayne State University	Learning objects Manufacturing curricula

NOTE: Two other coalitions, Academy and the Southern California Coalition for Education in Manufacturing Engineering (SCEME), which were funded for only three years from a technology reinvestment initiative, were less successful and had substantially different experiences. Only the six coalitions listed in Table 1 are considered in this report.

OVERVIEW

There has been a great deal of interest in a review of the EEC Program that would tell what was done, what worked, and what did not work. The National Academy of Engineering (NAE) requested a concise overview of the program to support its Engineer of 2020 Project, which will define how engineering in the twenty-first century will be refashioned. To assist NAE, we consider results from the EEC Program through four different "lenses":

- **Content.** Through this lens we describe new topics that might be included in engineering curricula.
- **Expectations.** We chose the word "expectations" instead of outcomes, objectives, goals, student outcomes, learning objectives, assessments, or evaluations, all of which might have preconceived meanings that could interfere with an objective description of expectations for engineering graduates. Issues associated with expectations include assessment and evaluation, because it must be determined if stated expectations have been met. In this respect, the expectation lens is similar to the testing lens for engineering design; testing requires not only specifications, but also methods of determining whether a product sample satisfies specifications. Other issues associated with expectations include retention of students and increased participation of underrepresented groups. Improvements in both areas were goals of the EEC Program.
- **Methodology.** The word "methodology" is used because readers might have preconceived ideas about the meaning of other words (e.g., pedagogy, teaching, classroom practice, and classroom approaches) that might interfere with an understanding of how expectations might be realized and/or improved. Issues associated with the methodology lens include pedagogy, lectures versus more active student engagement, and instructional technology.
- **Systemic reform.** This is the most complex lens, and the most fundamental, because significant investments were made in hopes that reforms initiated in a particular EEC would have major positive effects well beyond the schools directly involved in that coalition.

The Content Lens

Content addresses questions such as new topics for engineering curricula and in what order topics should be presented. Questions about content can often be answered by textbooks. The EEC Program contributed surprisingly little new content. EECs invested comparatively little effort in adding topics to engineering curricula or in reordering existing subject matter. This may seem surprising considering that new technological areas (e.g., information technology, biotechnology, nanotechnology, sustainable engineering, etc.) are continuously emerging. Various explanations might be offered for the comparatively small investments in content.

First, engineering curricula have reached topical capacity. Thus, adding new topics at this point would require eliminating other topics, and reaching consensus on which topics are the most important is a difficult and contentious process. Second, EECs were intended to address questions associated with engineering education as a system; topical additions and/or deletions raise questions for individual disciplines, rather than for engineering as a whole. Third, adding new topics may not have appeared to be as pressing a challenge as increasing the number of engineering graduates, raising retention rates for students already in engineering, increasing the percentages of students from traditionally underrepresented groups, such as white women and minorities, and improving students' capabilities in communications, teamwork, problem solving, ethics, engineering design, project management, and lifelong learning. Changes in content would not have addressed these needs.

Given that the results of the EEC program in terms of content were comparatively small and given the preeminence attached to content by people associated with engineering, some might conclude that the EEC Program contributed little to engineering education. We hope that conclusion will be reversed when the program is looked at through the other lenses.

The Expectations Lens

Each EEC first articulated expectations for graduates of engineering education programs, refined them to the point that assessment methods could be formulated and implemented, and then shared their expertise and experience associated with these processes nationwide.

EEC contributions viewed through the expectations lens will be examined in three categories: the performance and capabilities of engineering graduates; the participation of underrepresented groups in engineering; and the number of engineering graduates.

The Performance and Capabilities of Engineering Graduates

The EECs made major contributions to the formulation, refinement, and assessment of student outcomes beyond the traditional focus on knowledge and applications of engineering science. The EECs focused significant attention on engineering design and teamwork. In almost every design activity created by the EECs, students worked in teams. Most of the partner institution in the ECSEL coalition developed and subsequently institutionalized a first-year engineering course that emphasized engineering design as a process and enabled student teams to engineer meaningful prototypes. Multidisciplinary design, in which engineering majors from many disciplines, and sometimes other majors, worked together on teams, was a key aspect of activities developed by SUCCEED; partner institutions developed capstone courses in which multidisciplinary teams developed solutions to problems posed by external clients. SUCCEED partners also developed design courses for first-year engineering students. Many institutions in all of the EECs developed team projects as integral parts of both first-year integrated curricula and individual courses.

Another goal of numerous institutions was integration, that is, the linking of concepts among courses to enable students to transfer knowledge to novel situations, both in their undergraduate courses and in their subsequent careers. Coalition partner institutions initiated numerous integrated-curriculum pilot projects, especially in first-year curricula. Based on their experiences with these pilot programs, many then proceeded to institutionalize integrated curricula that combined learning communities, student teams, and active/cooperative learning. However, some unique features of the pilot projects (e.g., specific topical rearrangements) did not transfer to the institutionalized versions either because of perceived increases in faculty workload or resistance to changes in the institutional culture (e.g., "That's not the way we do it here.").

In developing multidisciplinary design and integrated curricular projects, the EEC institutions had to create much of the required infrastructure, such as (1) faculty teams and interactions that crossed departmental and college boundaries and (2) assessment processes to measure the outcomes of these unique programs. Even though many interdepartmental and intercollegiate boundaries were bridged for pilot programs, sustaining those bridges proved to be challenging.

Assessments of student outcomes in engineering design courses, multidisciplinary design courses, and integrated curricula require careful definitions of observable student behaviors (e.g., team skills, design skills, multidisciplinary design skills, communication skills, and linking of concepts) and work products. Once the definitions had been established, assessment instruments and processes had to be developed. The EECs made progress on these challenging tasks, but they had to start from ground zero in every area except communication skills and team skills. Their efforts to improve assessments of student outcomes were in step with ABET's development and implementation of outcomes-based accreditation. However, assessment processes for many outcomes related to engineering design and practice were still not sufficiently developed for widespread implementation or for the acquisition and interpretation of critical data.

Recent results of continuing research have yielded concept maps and assessment instruments for engineering design and metacognitive control that can be used to estimate performance. For example, engineering-science concept inventories to estimate conceptual understanding are being beta-tested across the nation. Concept maps, in which students are asked to produce graphical representations of concepts and their interrelationships, are being refined into instruments that can be scored and used to assess structured knowledge of concepts. Instruments are also being developed, tested, and adopted to assess knowledge and skills in engineering design. The coalitions made outstanding progress in these innovative directions and in creating an infrastructure that could support continued progress. However, a tremendous amount of work remains to be done.

Increased Participation of Underrepresented Groups

One of the expectations for the EEC Program was to increase the participation of students from underrepresented groups, such as white women and some racial/ethnic minorities. Efforts to increase the percentages of these groups can be divided into three categories:

(1) outreach efforts to increase the number of students from under-represented groups in engineering; (2) efforts to work with students from under-represented groups who enroll in engineering to improve their success rate; and (3) curricular reforms that promote success in engineering for all students, including students from underrepresented groups.

Examples of outreach programs include: sending engineering students into K-12 schools to provide information and demonstrations of the nature of engineering; working with K-12 students on weekends or during the summer to promote their understanding of the nature of engineering; and working with K-12 teachers and/or guidance counselors to improve their understanding of the nature of engineering and career opportunities for their students. Examples of "success efforts" included: peer mentoring programs; summer bridge programs to provide support for students during the transition from high school to college; academic success programs to improve study skills, essential technical and nontechnical skills, and social skills that are vital to academic success, especially for students from underrepresented groups; and programs on women in engineering and minorities in engineering.

Although outreach and success efforts by EECs did increase participation and the retention of students from underrepresented groups, they were not unique to EEC participating institutions and did not promote systemic reform in engineering education. In addition, most outreach and success efforts did not involve engineering faculty members who were not engaged in constructing these programs. As a result, they remained uninformed about research on underrepresented groups in engineering, rationales for outreach and success programs, and the successes of such programs. Consequently, these programs have not changed the learning environments in which the vast majority of students study engineering.

Efforts at curricular reform were based on the understanding that recruiting members of underrepresented groups into engineering curricula fashioned by white males and then working with them to encourage their success did not address a basic problem—the curricula in place in 1990 did not have the attributes that would stimulate interest and promote the success of students from underrepresented groups, or, in fact, all students. The curricula did not provide students with experience with engineering practice and artifacts, did not build links between abstract concepts and real-life tasks, and did not build connec-

.tions among students or between students and faculty, which have been demonstrated to increase retention.

Many of the above-mentioned innovative curricular efforts to promote nontraditional student outcomes did have these attributes: they encouraged the development and institutionalization of first-year engineering design courses, design courses in which student teams worked on projects for external clients (both for-profit and nonprofit), and integrated curricula. More important, engineering faculty members were actively engaged in the conceptualization, design, implementation, and, in many cases, assessment of curricular reforms. Even though many of these pilot initiatives demonstrated improvements in the retention rate of underrepresented groups, institutional barriers and the absence of the necessary assessment infrastructure limited their success.

Increasing the Number of Engineering Graduates

The outreach programs, success programs, and curricular reforms initiated to increase the participation of underrepresented groups were also used to increase the overall retention of engineering majors. Typically, if a student completes the first two years of an engineering program, he or she will graduate with an engineering degree. Therefore, efforts to improve retention have been focused on the first two years of engineering programs, and faculty members have been actively engaged in those initiatives.

Pilot curricular initiatives demonstrated an increase in the retention of engineering majors, and many curricular pilots were used as the basis for renewing curricula for all engineering students. However, institutional barriers and the absence of an assessment infrastructure limited the success of curricular reforms.

THE METHODOLOGY LENS

Based on the foregoing description of the expectations for the EEC Program and the degree to which those expectations have been achieved, we can turn now to a brief overview of the approaches used to meet those expectations. Viewed through the methodology lens, we can group the contributions of the EECs into six categories: active, experiential learning environments; student teams; instructional technologies; integration across disciplinary boundaries; assessment; and faculty development.

Active, Experiential Learning Environments

Every coalition consistently advocated and implemented learning environments and approaches in which students (1) were more actively engaged than taking notes, (2) focused on problems, design challenges, and artifacts in addition to concepts, and (3) often worked with other students to understand and complete assigned tasks. Specific innovations that illustrate these learning environments include first-year engineering design courses that focus on design challenges; artifact dissection, in which students disassemble engineered artifacts; problem-based learning environments, in which students start with a problem instead of a concept; cooperative learning environments, in which students work together to achieve learning objectives; and multidisciplinary design projects that bring together students from different educational backgrounds.

Student Teams

Every EEC consistently emphasized using student teams in many different learning situations, including design projects and engineering-science courses. However, many questions remain about how to assess whether teamwork skills and team leadership skills were improved.

Instructional Technologies

Every EEC consistently advocated greater use of instructional technology in many different forms. A paper on this topic by Donald Falkenburg, Project Director of the Greenfield Coalition, is included in this Appendix (p. 69).

Integration Across Disciplinary Boundaries

Although the importance of students linking concepts across disciplines was not always recognized at the beginning of the EEC Program, many EEC projects began to emphasize integration as the program evolved. Numerous first-year integrated pilot programs were implemented, and many have evolved into sustained, institutionalized programs that have fostered the development of student learning communities.

Assessment

The infrastructure to support assessments of curricular innovations, especially on the scale implemented in many EEC projects, was virtually nonexistent when the EEC Program was initiated. The critical role of assessment was recognized only gradually. The adoption of the new Engineering Criteria by ABET in the mid-1990s was pivotal to the near-universal recognition of the importance of assessment and stimulated the development of an infrastructure to support assessments of critical, nontraditional learning outcomes.

Every EEC invested substantial resources both to assess its initiatives and to support the further development of assessment instruments and processes, such as Team Developer, the mining of student-information databases, and concept inventories. However, despite the outcomes-based ABET Engineering Criteria and efforts by the coalitions, the infrastructure for the assessment of critical capabilities (e.g., design, problem-solving, lifelong learning) has not yet matured to the point of supporting systemic reform in engineering education.

Faculty Development

In the beginning, faculty development did not appear on the action agendas of the EECs. When the importance of faculty development was recognized, about midway through the program, all of the EECs initiated programs to address faculty development; subsequent assessments of these programs suggest that they did have some effect. For example, surveys of faculty by SUCCEED suggested that the value of active learning environments was more widely recognized.

THE SYSTEMIC REFORM LENS

In terms of systemic reform, the EEC Program yielded two significant lessons. First, the dissemination of the results of engineering education research and development is far more difficult than was initially understood. Second, the culture of engineering education is sustained by engineering faculty members, and systemic reform will require cultural change. However, defining the nature of cultural change and, therefore, faculty change, as well as initiatives to promote cultural change, proved to be elusive.

The Dissemination Challenge

Based on the EEC experience, the traditional means of disseminating research results (e.g., conference papers, journal articles, etc.) are insufficient to catalyze systemic reform for several reasons. First, whereas the intended audience for a discipline-specific research publication is researchers actively involved in work in the same or closely related areas, the intended audience for a publication by one or more EEC is the entire engineering education community. However, only a small percentage of engineering faculty members regularly read engineering education publications. In addition, even those who do, read only a small percentage of the articles published. As a result, the EECs discovered that a large percentage of the engineering education community was unaware of the work they had done or the results they had achieved, even years after the results had been presented several times. Second, each publication tended to document work that had been done and the results in a particular institutional context. Most traditional publications did not include directions for implementation of the approach in other contexts or provide resources for faculty members who might want to adapt a particular EEC project.

As problems with traditional dissemination mechanisms were realized, the EECs tried more innovative approaches, three of which are described below: websites; workshops; and summaries. Project web sites are excellent repositories of information about the work of the coalitions, and faculty members searching for particular information can find useful resources at one or more of the coalition web sites. However, these web sites only provide information to faculty members actively searching for resources related to innovations in engineering education. In addition, navigating and finding the desired resources at a coalition web site can be challenging.

Several coalitions developed interactive workshops that could be held on campuses, at national conferences, such as those of the American Society for Engineering Education, Frontiers in Education, and the American Institute of Chemical Engineers, and at conferences organized by coalitions. These workshops synthesize work from several projects and offer participants an opportunity to explore the results in depth. However, the number of participants that can be reached through a workshop is small compared to the potential audience. In addition, although workshops were offered at no cost to host campuses, surprisingly few took advantage of the offer. Four Share the Future Conferences, which consisted almost entirely of interactive workshops, were offered by the Foundation, Gateway, and SUCCEED coalitions. Participants at each conference praised the quality and breadth of the material covered at the workshops; however, the participating audiences were too small to justify additional conferences.

The third innovative dissemination mechanism was compact summaries synthesizing the results of particular educational innovations. One-page introductions that could be read in 10 to 20 minutes and mini-documents that could be read in less than an hour provided faculty members with an opportunity to learn about innovations in engineering education with a small investment of precious time. More than 20,000 copies of compact summaries by the Foundation Coalition have been downloaded from its web site. Given the small investment in reading a compact summary, however, the only anticipated result is greater receptivity to future encounters with the subject. So, despite innovative and diligent initiatives, the dissemination of results of educational research and development remains a challenge.

The Cultural and Faculty Change Challenge

The importance of cultural change emerged as the EEC Program shifted its focus from the development of models of curricular renewal on partner campuses to the catalysis of systemic reform. However, a clear understanding of the characteristics of cultural change and processes for achieving it did not emerge. Researchers who have studied cultural change suggest that the challenges are much more extensive than is usually recognized. Seel (2000) suggests that cultural change in engineering education will be achieved only when the nature of the conversation about engineering education has changed. Eckel and Kezar (2003) suggest that transforming engineering education will require that the majority of engineering faculty members change the way they think about engineering education. If these researchers are correct, then the magnitude of the challenge is apparent. The assumptions and mechanisms that sustain the current system of engineering education, and higher education in general, are more complex than is implied in simple admonitions, such as "research is rewarded while teaching is not" and "faculty members need to learn more about education research and methods."

Efforts to date have not clarified the nature, intensity, and expertise that will be required to develop a "conversation" that will lead to systemic reform in engineering education. Dee Hock (1999) states that it took two years of regular, intense conversations among experts in the banking industry to hammer out the principles for the foundation of Visa International. Because engineering education is a much larger and more complex enterprise than banking, longer, more intensive, more inclusive, and more informed conversations will be necessary to establish a foundation for sustainable, systemic reform.

The length of time required to achieve widespread, sustained change must be matched to the extent, breadth, and depth of the challenge. For example, in the classic *Diffusion of Innovations*, Rogers (1995) noted that it required a decade before almost all Iowa farmers adopted hybrid corn. And the case for changing to hybrid corn (higher yields with no changes in farming practices) was much more compelling than the current arguments for reform in engineering education. Therefore, it might take two to four times as long to achieve systemic reform in engineering education. Lessons from other efforts to bring about cultural change might also be enlightening.

CONCLUSION

The EEC Program demonstrated that engineering faculty members can construct out-of-the-box, effective models for curricular and systemic reform, and assessment data indicate that they lead to increased retention and improved student learning. However, the EEC Program also demonstrated that institutional and cultural barriers to change are more complex, intricate, and subtle than is often appreciated and that innovative models for reform are seldom enough to overcome the challenges to institutionalizing change. In addition, the program demonstrated that effective models, even when well supported by assessment data, do not catalyze systemic reform. To achieve that goal, resources matched to the extent, complexity, and dynamics of the system of engineering education must be assembled and deployed through intense, informed, and sustained conversation.

REFERENCES

Eckel, P.D. and A. Kezar. 2003. Taking the Reins: Institutional Transformation in Higher Education. Westport, Conn.: Praeger.

Hock, D.W. 1999. Birth of the Chaordic Age. San Francisco, Calif.: Berrett-Koehler.

Rogers, E.M. 1995. Diffusion of Innovations, 4th ed. New York: Free Press.

Seel, R. 2000. Culture and complexity: New insights on organizational change. Organizations and People 7(2): 2–9.

Designing from a Blank Slate: The Development of the Initial Olin College Curriculum

Sherra E. Kerns, Richard K. Miller, and David V. Kerns
Franklin W. Olin College of Engineering

Olin College is an independent institution conceived and primarily funded by the F.W. Olin Foundation. The college, located in Needham, Massachusetts, on about 70 acres of land adjacent to Babson College, was chartered in 1997 by the Massachusetts Board of Higher Education to offer a B.S. in mechanical engineering, electrical and computer engineering, and engineering. Conceived as a residential undergraduate institution focusing on the education of engineers, Olin College was charged by the foundation with exploring, testing, and implementing innovative engineering curricula and addressing what the National Science Foundation (NSF) and others have identified as systemic issues with existing engineering education.

The college is entering its third year of teaching programs for credit; for the preceding two years the faculty worked full time on inventing the curriculum. The short-term enrollment target is 300 students; the campus is designed for an ultimate enrollment of 600 to 650 students. A fundamental objective of the F.W. Olin Foundation is that Olin College offer all of its admitted students a four-year, merit-based tuition scholarship, not just for the first few years but in perpetuity. Admission to the college is highly competitive, and a student/faculty ratio of fewer than 10 to 1 will be maintained (the ratio will be much lower in the early years).

Although Olin College is completely independent of nearby Babson College, the two institutions have established a strong collaborative relationship that enables the sharing of certain facilities and services. Olin students routinely take a variety of courses in liberal arts and business at Babson, as well as a wide range of courses through cross-registration agreements at nearby Wellesley College and Brandeis University.

Olin College is distinctive in several ways. First, the college is not organized with traditional academic departments. Instead, the faculty operates as a single interdisciplinary group, and faculty offices are assigned with no regard to discipline, so there is a mix of faculty backgrounds on every hallway to encourage interdisciplinary thinking. The steady-state faculty count will approach 40 in the near term. Faculty employment relationships are based on renewable contracts rather than a traditional tenure system.

A primary objective of Olin College is to develop a culture of innovation and continuous improvement, with an enhanced entrepreneurial focus. In the fall of 2000 (prior to the arrival of the first students), the college established a two-year strategic plan in pursuit of this objective. The resulting plan, Invention 2000, reflects a comprehensive effort to rethink all aspects of an educational institution, including curriculum, student life, administration and finance, admission, development, and college governance. In each of these areas, a deliberate, four-stage plan consisting of a period of discovery (investigation of best practices), invention, development, and testing was executed.

An important aspect of the plan was the Olin Partners Program. To establish the initial curriculum, Olin College decided it would be beneficial to invite a group of students to help brainstorm and test concepts. In some respects, these students were considered partners in the development of portions of the curriculum and student life programs. In the spring of 2001, 30 Olin student partners were recruited; they arrived on campus on August 23, 2001. These students were involved in a unique academic program consisting of development and testing of components of the curriculum and other programs involving student life, community service, and relations with nearby colleges.

Their program was organized into six modules, either four or five weeks each, and included a four-week trip to France to investigate international aspects of the program on the campus of Georgia Tech Lorraine in Metz. Each of the four 4-week modules was used to test an aspect of the curriculum. The partners received "non-degree" credit for the year. The first freshman class of 75 arrived in fall 2002. The class consisted of the 30 student partners (who will spend a total of five years to complete their B.S. degrees), 15 "virtual Olin partners," who received deferred admission from the Partners Program, and 30 additional new students.

Before the first employee was hired at Olin College, the F.W. Olin Foundation began planning an entirely new campus consisting of about 500,000 square feet in eight new buildings. The first four buildings, completed in the fall of 2002, include Olin Center (faculty offices, administrative offices, a library, a computer center, and an auditorium), Campus Center (a dining hall, student-life offices, a central heating and cooling plant), an academic center (27 major classrooms, teaching, or research laboratories [about 1,100 square feet each], and numerous smaller teaching and laboratory spaces), and the first residence hall (188 beds in double rooms, each with a private bathroom); the new construction totals about 300,000 square feet. Subsequent construction will be phased, as needed, and will include additional residence halls and another academic building. The second residence hall is under construction and is scheduled to be completed during the coming academic year.

In early 1999, the Olin Foundation hired the founding president, Richard K. Miller, who hired the founding leadership: David V. Kerns, provost; Sherra E. Kerns, vice president for innovation and research; Stephen P. Hannabury, vice president for administration and finance; and Duncan C. Murdoch, vice president for external relations and enrollment. The founding faculty was then recruited by the provost and explicitly charged with leading the development of the new curriculum. The college looked for faculty members with a passion for undergraduate teaching and innovation in engineering education. However, because Olin College is not just a teaching institution, faculty members are also expected to maintain a high level of research, innovative curriculum development, entrepreneurship, creation of intellectual property, and other creative activities. This kind of intellectual vitality will keep faculty members current in their fields.

The provost was looking for faculty with the following characteristics (Kerns, 1999):

- a passion for teaching and education and a strong commitment to improving student's lives
- strong evidence of creativity through research, publications, inventions, entrepreneurship, commercialization of technology,

new course or curriculum developments, innovative engineering pedagogy, etc.

- evidence of integration of creativity (as identified above) into the classroom
- a willingness to work as part of a team, to accept others' ideas, to "partner," to lead, or to follow
- a desire to stay current and to reflect current developments in teaching and in creative endeavors
- the potential for "nationally visible achievements" through any of the creativity channels above
- a willingness to take reasonable risks to make a significant impact

INVENTION 2000

Invention 2000 was proposed by President Miller as a blueprint for developing all of the academic and operational aspects of the Franklin W. Olin College of Engineering. Starting with a clean slate, the plan includes an outline of an intensive two-year project of unprecedented scope to produce (1) innovative educational processes for preparing the next generation of leaders in a technological society and (2) institutional policies establishing a commitment to continuous improvement and innovation. The document includes plans for intense efforts on all aspects of the college. However, only the section dealing with the development of the academic curriculum will be discussed here. Because the project was funded by the F.W. Olin Foundation as part of the founding gift, the faculty and staff were able to devote two full years of effort to the project without the distractions of teaching responsibilities. The following excerpt is from *Invention 2000,* which is available on the Olin website:

This project will involve the founding faculty, educational consultants, and students in the creation of innovative engineering curricula, which simultaneously address all major challenges identified by the National Science Foundation. These, together with several additional features, will distinguish Olin College from other engineering colleges. These anticipated distinctive features of the curricula include the combination of a rigorous science and mathematics core, an integrated project-based design component, a firm grounding in the fundamentals of business and entrepreneurship, a strong international component, a vigorous co-curricular component which makes good use of strengths in humanities and social sciences at nearby colleges, and an emphasis on student service to society and a lifestyle of philanthropy.

The project will be addressed in four sequential stages. For brevity, these stages will be referred to as (1) discovery, (2) invention, (3) development, and (4) test. The general nature of the activities intended to occur during each phase is as follows. During the **discovery phase**, research into "best practices" at other institutions will take place. Deliberate efforts will be made to visit other campuses, host visitors from other campuses, obtain advice from knowledgeable consultants, and obtain broad knowledge of the various successful approaches in use today. During the **invention phase**, knowledge of best practices will be applied in a creative way to the problem of inventing an overall vision of the four-year educational experience. This will begin with a fundamental evaluation of educational goals and objectives and end with a comprehensive concept for obtaining balance in the overall curriculum. During the **development phase**, further refinement of the newly invented curriculum will take place in which the needed detail for the freshman year experience will be developed. This will result in a set of specific courses or educational experiences for teaching the freshmen in Fall 2002, as well as textbooks, laboratory experiments, reading materials, etc. Finally, during the **test phase**, the specific educational materials will be tested with the help of a small group of student "partners" who will be recruited specifically for this purpose and will help with INVENTION 2000 as part of a unique one-year experience at Olin College. Each of these stages will take from four to eight months, with the first (discovery) beginning in Fall 2000 and the last (test) ending in Summer 2002.

DEVELOPMENT OF THE CURRICULUM

The *Invention 2000* plan for curriculum development was initially executed primarily by faculty teams assigned to various activities. Faculty groups of two or three visited 31 colleges and universities and studied and reported on curricula at a wide range of institutions. They also visited (or hosted) more than 23 corporations and government agencies to explore corporate learning models and assess corporate values and needs in engineering education. In addition, consultants were brought to campus to discuss specific topics, and the results of the NSF coalition programs were reviewed in detail. The data were then compiled and discussed in a series of faculty meetings and off-campus retreats. With the arrival of the student partners, various teaching and learning concepts developed during the previous year were tested with "real" freshman-age students.

Several of the principles that emerged have stood the test of time and are still used to guide curricular discussions. One of these, the "Olin Triangle," was first proposed as a visual expression of Olin's goal to "educate the whole person" and "open doors to student possibilities" (see Figure 1). The Olin Triangle shows the three major dimensions of an Olin engineering education: (1) superb engineering; (2) a strong emphasis on art, design, creativity, and innovation; and (3) basics in business, entrepreneurship, ethics, and a spirit of philanthropy.

"Bold Goals" were developed by the founding faculty at one of the first off-campus retreats, in the fall of 2000. The Bold Goals summarized the curricular objectives at that time and are still used to guide curriculum development:

- hands-on design projects in every year
- authentic, ambitious capstone senior/advanced-student projects (representative of professional practice)

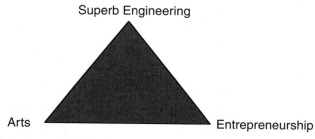

FIGURE 1 The Olin Triangle.

- experience working independently, as a member of a team, and as a leader of a team
- performance before an audience that includes experts
- international/intercultural immersion experience
- substantial constructive contribution to society
- ability to communicate logically and persuasively in spoken, written, numerical, and visual forms
- development of self-sufficient individuals able to articulate and activate a vision and bring it to fruition

All of these goals are to be accomplished in an environment of personal attention and concern.

Additional curricular objectives are listed below:

- demonstrate significant creative artistic expression
- aquire significant work experience in a corporate or business culture
- show ability to apply basic business practices necessary to bring a product to the marketplace

The many ways these goals could be implemented in real curricula were openly and widely debated for months. One of the realities of starting a college from a clean slate is that faculty groups are small, and there is a natural tendency for these groups to seek consensus. The college leadership was concerned, however, that consensus might close off discussions of truly innovative ideas and creative (sometimes wild) concepts that are "outside the box." Nevertheless, from the wide menu of possibilities, choices had to be made that would meet the realities of a four-year time constraint, Accrediting Board of Engineering and Technology (ABET) accreditation requirements, reasonable cost, and many other factors, at the same time, remaining true to the founding principles.

To move the selection process forward, the provost established the Curriculum Decision Making Board (CDMB), a group of five faculty members and one student partner. This group was charged with the task of describing the first Olin curriculum. Three of the five faculty members of the CDMB were elected by the faculty using a Copeland ballot, and two were appointed by the provost. The student partner was selected by the student government group. The members of the CDMB were Professors Steve Schiffman and Mike Moody (cochairs), Rob

Martello, Joanne Pratt, Mark Somerville, Jon Stolk, and Brian Storey; the student partner was Sean Munson. This group put forward the first detailed proposal for the Olin curriculum.

In the fall of 2002, Michael E. Moody joined Olin College as dean of the faculty and assumed direct leadership of the development of the Olin curriculum. Dean Moody created a successor group to CDMB, the Academic Recommendations Board, which currently oversees curricular modifications and changes. Although modifications are being introduced to the curriculum described below, most of the fundamental concepts and structure have not changed.

THE INITIAL OLIN CURRICULUM

For the last 20 years, NSF and the engineering community have been calling for systemic changes in engineering education:

- a shift from disciplinary to interdisciplinary approaches
- more emphasis on communication and teamwork skills
- more emphasis on the social, environmental, business, and political context of engineering
- improved capacity for lifelong learning
- more emphasis on engineering practice and design throughout the curriculum

In this section, we describe the "first fruits" of Olin's efforts to rethink engineering education—the first Olin curriculum, which was implemented in the fall of 2002. The curriculum combines best practices from many other institutions with new ideas and approaches. Because Olin is committed to continuous innovation and improvement, the curriculum described in this document represents only the "initial conditions" for continuous curriculum reviews and refinements that will never really end. As expected, improvements and adjustments are already being made.

CURRICULAR PHILOSOPHY

The founding principle of Olin College of Engineering is to prepare leaders who can predict, create, and manage the technologies of the future. Such leaders must have the following characteristics:

- a superb command of engineering fundamentals
- a broad perspective on the role of engineering in society
- the creativity to envision new solutions to problems
- the entrepreneurial skills to bring these visions to reality

The Olin curriculum is designed to give students all of these capabilities. Rigorous technical courses and hands-on projects throughout the curriculum require that students apply engineering concepts to real problems. Interdisciplinary courses and projects make explicit connections in the technical world and between engineering and society. Extensive design experiences, significant work in the arts and humanities, and an emphasis on original expression encourage students to develop and apply their creativity. Continuous use of teamwork, communication skills, and entrepreneurial thinking give students the tools they need to take their solutions from the research laboratory to the world at large.

The Olin curriculum consists of three phases (Figure 2): **foundation**, which emphasizes mastering and applying technical fundamentals

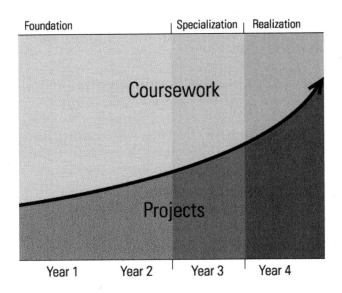

FIGURE 2 Structure of the Olin curriculum. Projects occupy an increasing proportion of the curriculum as students progress from foundation to specialization to realization.

in substantial engineering projects; **specialization**, in which students develop and apply in-depth knowledge in their chosen fields; and **realization**, in which students bring what they have learned to bear on problems approaching professional practice. In all three phases of the curriculum, students are engaged in interdisciplinary engineering projects that require them to put theory into practice, to put engineering in a larger context, and to develop teaming and management skills. As a student progresses, projects become increasingly open-ended and authentic. Students have significant flexibility in charting their path through the curriculum, but all students must demonstrate a mastery of required material through regular assessments.

The Foundation

Figure 3 illustrates the basic structure and requirements of the curricular "foundation," which encompasses approximately the first two years of a student's education. A central building block of the foundation is the **cohort** (a large block of coursework—equivalent to three conventional courses) taught by a multidisciplinary faculty team. The cohort combines two disciplinary topics with a large interdisciplinary project, thus requiring close coordination between the understanding of underlying disciplines and the application of this knowledge to real engineering problems. Cohorts also provide a logical environment for students to develop entrepreneurial skills, such as opportunity assessment and teamwork. Finally, cohorts address student choice—in a given semester, students can opt for one of three "flavors" of cohort.

For example, a student particularly interested in entrepreneurship might opt to pursue a given set of physics and math learning objectives while doing a related product-design and development project. An artistically inclined student might enroll in a cohort that uses kinetic sculpture to motivate and reinforce the same physics and math objectives. In some cases, cohorts combine two technical subjects (e.g., physics and mathematics); in other cases, cohorts emphasize context by combining technical with nontechnical material (e.g., materials science and business). In all cases, cohorts provide connections between subjects and bring theory into practice through projects.

Another prominent feature of the curriculum is the **sophomore design project** in the second semester of the sophomore year. Although students are engaged in design throughout the first two years through

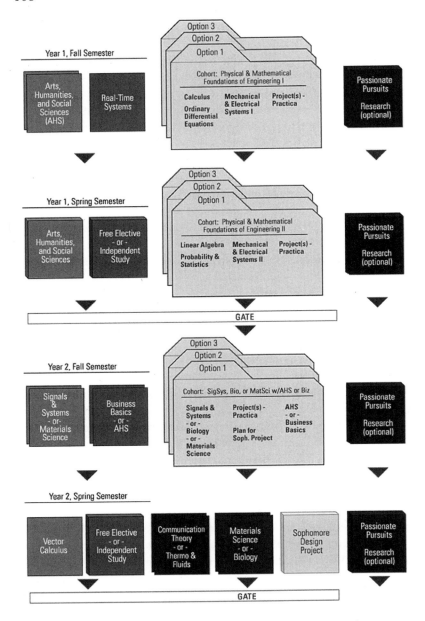

FIGURE 3 Illustration of the foundation. Although all students are required to meet the same learning objectives, they have many choices for doing so—free electives and an option structure in the cohorts.

the cohorts, the sophomore design project offers a significant opportunity for students to develop their own ideas, develop project implementation plans, and manage the process of bringing projects to fruition. Planning (i.e., team formation and proposal writing) for the design project begins in the first semester of the sophomore year.

To provide a context for their engineering studies, students will also take courses in the **arts, humanities, and social sciences.** In addition, in each semester of the foundation, students will participate in projects, practica (e.g., short, just-in-time learning experiences), and a required course on the basics of business to ensure that they have a solid grounding in **business and entrepreneurship.** In some cases, this course work will be connected directly to technical course work via projects—for example, students might combine a study of signals with a course on music theory and a project that focuses on building musical instruments. Alternatively, signals might be combined with a study of business and a project on opportunities in low-cost image processing. All students will graduate with some background in both business and the humanities. In addition, students will have the flexibility to choose which area they wan to emphasize.

Students' command of both theory and practice is evaluated at the end of each year during "**Gates,**" a week-long, institution-wide assessment period that includes written examinations, oral examinations, team exercises, and other forms of authentic assessment. Interdisciplinary by design, Gates forces students to synthesize material among classes and from one term to the next. Gates is designed to assess institutionally defined learning objectives, rather than objectives determined by a single instructor. By defining a desired outcome, but not the means by which it is to be achieved, Gates allows faculty members great flexibility in designing courses. Criteria-based assessment provides invaluable feedback to inform curricular innovation and, at the same time, ensures that students have met the learning objectives for the year.

To encourage student creativity and initiative, Olin encourages students to undertake **passionate pursuits.** Olin implemented this program to acknowledge students' passions—whether they are technical, artistic, or entrepreneurial—that are important to their personal and professional education and development. Some Olin students might use this opportunity to start a business with the support of an Olin/Babson hatchery; others might form a string quartet. Olin gives students the opportunity to pursue their passions independently by providing resources and formal recognition via non-degree credit. Students can also opt to pursue **independent study** and **research** as part of the Olin curriculum; space is provided for these activities—either as free electives each year or as passionate pursuits.

Specialization and Realization

Figure 4 shows the current concept for the third and fourth years of the curriculum, in which cohorts again play a significant role. **Specialization cohorts** might revolve around different application areas of

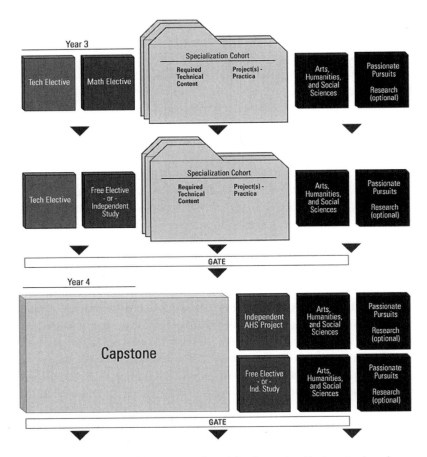

FIGURE 4 Illustration of the concept of specialization and realization. Students have a great amount of flexibility during years three and four.

interest. Each cohort option will link one course with a project; additional optional courses will add "flavors" to the project. For example, a biotech specialization cohort could connect a biology course with a project. Some students might take a computational science course as an optional elective and focus their project on bioinformatics. A second group might take entrepreneurship as the technical elective and focus on biotech start-ups. Such projects are compelling both for students and for prospective faculty, and they provide logical opportunities for corporate involvement.

The junior year will be the ideal time for **international study** and **corporate experience.** Because content in the specialization and realization years is defined by institutionally determined learning objectives and measured during Gates, students can easily design nontraditional means of achieving those objectives.

The final year at Olin will be focused on an ambitious **capstone project** that occupies at least half of the student's time for the semester. The precise structure of this capstone has not been entirely defined, but it will certainly look quite a bit like professional practice. Also in the final year, students will complete a **culminating project in the humanities.** In many cases, we imagine this project will be connected with the capstone project. Olin students are encouraged to pass the **Fundamentals of Engineering exam,** which is designed to encourage self-study skills, open the door to professional practice, and provide external validation of a student's proficiency.

ABET Requirements

The Olin curriculum is designed to satisfy the accreditation requirements of ABET. We believe that our focus on institution-wide learning objectives and our use of Gates to assess whether courses achieve desired outcomes and to promote improvement of the curriculum are entirely consistent with ABET's philosophy of assessment, evaluation, and improvement. The emphasis on interdisciplinary, hands-on design projects throughout the curriculum also meets ABET criteria. In addition, the curriculum is designed to satisfy ABET's mechanical engineering and electrical and computer engineering requirements through the specialization cohorts, which will address precise learning objectives.

Key Features of the Olin Curriculum

The Olin curriculum has a number of unique features that merit repeating:

- **Emphasis on engineering design, with substantial projects (20 percent to 60 percent of a student's time) every semester.** A defining feature of the Olin curriculum, these projects require that students apply math, science, and engineering principles to real problems, consider engineering in a social context, and develop entrepreneurial skills. Olin students will graduate with extensive experience in applying theoretical knowledge to real problems.
- **Objective-driven education based on assessments.** Olin's curriculum is based on institutionally defined learning objectives that are assessed every year by the **institution** and by **outside evaluators**—not just by the instructor for a given course. This commitment is critical to Olin's mission of innovation and improvement.
- **Breaking of disciplinary boundaries.** Through interdisciplinary courses and projects, students learn the value of thinking in non-traditional ways. Olin's decision not to establish academic departments will further this goal.
- **Emphasis on teamwork.** Faculty members work on teams in the cohort system and via other team-teaching opportunities. Students learn "teaming" skills, both formally and through extensive teamwork on projects.
- **Flexibility and accountability.** The objective-driven cohort system provides flexibility with accountability for instructors. Students shape their educations through learning plans that enable them to determine their short-term and long-term learning goals and to make sure they meet these goals. Students also have choices in subject matter—in their passionate pursuits and their projects.

In summary, the initial Olin curriculum was created in response to calls for changes in engineering education. In the spirit of continuous improvement, the initial curriculum is already undergoing change, and this process will continue as the curriculum constantly evolves. The freedom of starting with a blank slate, combined with excellent students, faculty, leadership, and resources, have provided Olin a unique opportunity to develop new ideas and a culture that welcomes innovation. By teaching entrepreneurship, social context, creativity with design, and superb engineering, Olin intends to provide a learning environment suited to the acquisition and development of knowledge, skills, and attitudes that will enable Olin graduates to be productive contributors throughout their lives.

ACKNOWLEDGMENT

The authors wish to thank the Olin College faculty for help with this paper.

REFERENCES

Kerns, D. 1999. Characteristics of Founding Faculty. Needham, Mass.: Olin College.
Miller, R. 2000. Invention 2000. Available online at *http://www.olin.edu.*

Patterns in the History of Engineering Education Reform: A Brief Essay

Bruce E. Seely
Michigan Technological University

Engineering education has been the subject of more studies and reviews, formal and informal, than any other domain of professional education. Indeed, one might argue that engineering education has undergone continuous reform since college classrooms challenged apprenticeships and hands-on training in the last third of the nineteenth century. In the pages of the *Journal of Engineering Education,* which was launched by the Society for the Promotion of Engineering Education in 1893, one can track the ongoing debates about the nature and shape of engineering education. In addition, regular reports were issued on the state of the field at intervals of 10 to 15 years beginning with the Mann Report of 1918, which initiated the self-study process (ASEE, 1968; Grinter, 1956; Hammond, 1940; Jackson, 1939b; Mann, 1918; MIT Center for Policy Alternatives, 1975; NRC, 1986, 1989; SPEE, 1930, 1934).

The present meeting sponsored by the National Academy of Engineering is the most recent addition to the process. This history suggests that there is more self-awareness in the engineering community than in most other professional communities about the educational enterprise that prepares new members to enter the profession. The continuous conversations among engineering faculty members, professional and practicing engineers (especially in leading societies, such as the American Society of Civil Engineers, the Institute of Electrical and Electronics Engineers, the American Society of Mechanical Engineers, and the

American Institute of Chemical Engineers), and executives in the firms, businesses, and corporations that employ engineers have revolved around a few basic issues. Considering the enormous changes that have taken place in technology and in society at large since 1875, this continuity is striking. The intent of this brief essay is to identify the main currents in various reform movements.

The dominant issue has involved the content of engineering curricula, including the relationship between theory and practice, the length of engineering education, and the nature and structure of general education courses. Issues that reflect influences from society at large touch on the general goals and social expectations for engineering and on who should be an engineer.

THE CONTENT OF ENGINEERING CURRICULA

It is a truism that engineering education is a product of history. Yet, it is worth taking a moment to remember that until the end of the nineteenth century, the primary means by which a young man became an engineer was through a hands-on apprenticeship in a machine shop, at a drawing board, behind a transit, or on a construction site. Although educational institutions played a larger role than is often recognized by providing courses and certificates, and a handful of institutions developed full-blown curricula and degree programs, it was not until after the Civil War, when the Morrill Act led to the establishment of land-grant schools, that the dominant pattern of engineering education shifted from shop floors to classrooms (Reynolds, 1992). The formation of the Society for the Promotion of Engineering Education at the World's Columbian Exposition in Chicago in 1893 ratified this development (Reynolds and Seely, 1993).

A variety of factors influenced this transition. A major factor was the steady emergence of new technologies that defied commonsense, hands-on approaches to development and operation. Electrical and chemical technologies increasingly required that engineers be grounded in basic science—and in the case of alternating current, have a knowledge of mathematics—to develop and improve devices and systems in these fields. Thomas Edison, despite his attempts to appear as a trial-and-error inventor, maintained one of the best scientific libraries in the United States and routinely employed Ph.D.-holding scientists from Europe (Hughes, 1989). Similarly, the design and construction of the alternating-current generators for the hydroelectric complex at Niagara Falls in the 1890s owed much to European engineers because most Americans did not have sufficient background in physics and mathematics to design these devices (Hunter, 1979; Kline, 1984). Charles Steinmetz—a European immigrant working at General Electric in those years—was one who spoke out for educational changes to keep up with new technologies (Kline, 1992).

Another factor that influenced the shift to college education was the emerging patterns of middle-class America. Engineering was only one of the professions taking shape at this time; others included medicine, law, economics, and even history. These professional groups had several beliefs in common: that scientific knowledge was essential to the improvement of the nation; that people with scientific expertise should be given political and moral authority, as well as the social status that comes with that authority; and finally that the best way to gain expertise was through a university education.

The leaders of the engineering profession in the last quarter of the nineteenth century had an acute sensitivity to their lack of social position—at times to the point of an inferiority complex. Engineers frequently asked when they would get the respect they deserved for designing, operating, and maintaining the large systems on which Americans increasingly depended, ranging from water and power systems in cities to massive bridges and railroad networks. Eager to acquire the same prestige as other professions, engineers embraced college classrooms as the best approach to education, a decision that the demands of technologies reinforced (Calvert, 1967; Jackson, 1939a; Layton, 1971; Stine, 1984–1985).

But determining the nature, shape, and content of the classroom experience proved a contentious issue that took time to resolve (and is still being debated). A number of complex issues were involved, of which the most delicate seemed to be finding a balance between hands-on knowledge of devices and systems and a theoretical and scientific grasp of nature and mathematics (Seely, 1999). Over time, more emphasis was placed on an analytical style of engineering that emphasized science, especially mathematical expression (usually labeled engineering science) and less on the hands-on, empirical approach that stressed engineering design. But early debates were loud and prolonged, despite calls for changes as early as the 1880s by leading engineers, such as Robert Thurston of Cornell. The most famous study of engineering education—the Wickenden report of the 1920s—also called for less hands-on specialization and more general preparation in math and science (Wickenden, 1927).

The change in emphasis gained momentum after European engineers who arrived here after 1920 demonstrated the practical utility of mathematics in modern engineering sciences applied to practical problems, such as vibration and dynamic movement in machinery, the strength of materials, fluid dynamics in aviation and maritime engineering, and stresses in pavement slabs and dams. Even so, it wasn't until the 1950s, when the Grinter report (1956) again emphasized such knowledge and the federal government decided to fund fundamental research (as opposed to "applied" research) and unleashed an avalanche of money for university programs, that American engineering schools almost universally adopted engineering science as the core of engineering education.

The far-reaching ramifications of this change included the first significant focus on graduate education in engineering schools—especially at the Ph.D. level. Research programs, which had always been small and oriented more toward preparing students to understand research than toward generating new knowledge, assumed substantially more importance in the eyes of college and university administrators. Until this time, engineering faculty members were expected to have experience in the real world—usually in industry.

The new emphasis on federally funded research (more than 70 percent of university research was funded by the government) severed the tight linkage between engineering faculty and business corporations. The change was so complete that by the late 1960s practicing engineers were complaining that the pendulum had swung too far toward theoretical concerns, that engineering graduates lacked problem-solving capabilities, and that engineering faculty and practicing engineers spoke entirely different languages. Pressure began to build to redress the balance and restore design to engineering curricula and to rebuild ties between business and industry and engineering faculty. At the same time, the federal share of research funding declined or at least held steady (depending on the field) from the 1970s onward. In the 1990s, engineering curricula underwent major changes driven by the accreditation process overseen by the Accreditation Board for Engineering and Technology (ABET), with substantial support from American industry

(ABET, 2005; Covert, 1992; Curry, 1991; Dixon, 1991; Kerr and Pipes, 1987; Masi, 1995).

The proper balance between science, engineering science, and design is only one of the issues engineers and engineering educators have debated at length over the last 125 years. Other issues focused on the content of engineering curricula, such as how long an engineering education ought to last. Early on, the basic question of how long an engineer needed to go to school had attracted significant attention. The outcome was largely settled by adopting the pattern of four years of schooling that had become firmly entrenched at most American colleges. The weak preparation of many incoming students, however, forced some variations from the norm. For example, Cornell, the leading American engineering school by the 1880s, was determined to maintain high standards. To that end, Cornell established a preparatory academy for students who lacked solid backgrounds in math or science.

The pressures posed by new technologies also kept the length-of-study issue alive. After 1900, the problem became fitting the required material for all of the new fields and topics into existing curricula. The division of engineering into a large number of fields with specialized subdisciplines was one way to keep up with rapid technological change. New areas of study included industrial engineering, and subfields emerged in automotive, aeronautical, highway, radio, and municipal engineering and so forth.

Even these adjustments, however, did not eliminate the sense that a well-rounded, well-educated engineer had to know more and more. The slow acceptance of engineering science was one factor in the growing logjam, because fundamentals were given less emphasis than detailed knowledge of the undergraduate's specialty field. As new technologies burst onto the scene, each requiring new courses, engineering faculties almost continuously debated what to leave in and what to remove from the curriculum (Baker, 1900; Landreth, 1906).

Another potential solution was to add a year of course work. This idea was regularly discussed after 1900 as faculty members attempted to keep their particular courses in the educational program (Derleth, 1909; Fletcher, 1909; Humphries, 1913; Magruder, 1909; Marburg, 1902; Marvin, 1901; Swain, 1913; Turneaure, 1909).

After World War II, however, pressures on the curriculum reached a new level of intensity. The emergence of new military technologies, such as radar and atomic bombs, had resulted in kudos for physicists, leading many engineers—notably Stanford's Frederick Terman—to press for more math, physics, and engineering science for all students.

To ensure that engineers would never again lag behind physicists, degrees were offered in engineering science and engineering physics. New fields, such as nuclear engineering, computer science, and interdisciplinary materials science were evidence of how the new approaches to engineering would unfold. Three schools decided that the only way to ease the demands on students was to lengthen the curriculum to five years. Cornell, Ohio State, and Minnesota made the switch, promising that their graduates would be much better prepared for the new world of engineering. Their competitors contended that in four full years, students could do the same work and be employed a whole year sooner. All three schools quietly ended the experiment after only a few years (Cornell University Archives, 1948).

Ironically, almost every engineering college moved toward a post-war curriculum that meant engineering students spent nearly five years in school. This led Eric Walker, dean of engineering at Penn State in the late 1940s and president of that school from 1956 to 1971, to press for change. Walker was aware that every other profession required a graduate degree for admission to professional status. As president of the American Society of Engineering Education in the mid-1960s, Walker launched the Goals Study (Walker and Nead, 1966)—another review of the state of engineering education—an intensely controversial report that proposed addressing overloaded curricula by instituting a generalized undergraduate degree and reserving specialization for the master's level (an idea that Dartmouth adopted and has practiced for decades).

Toward the end of his life, Walker argued that, given the importance of technology to modern society, this change would allow engineering to become the "liberal arts degree" of the twenty-first century. By not specializing, undergraduates would have time for a broad education that would prepare them for leadership positions in society and business. By the 1990s, discussions about the relationship of undergraduate and graduate work in engineering were under way in a number of venues (Van Dam, 1990; Walker, 1989).

Walker's line of thinking was in keeping with the other main issue confronting engineers concerned with reforming the content of engineering curricula—the place and shape of general education. The issue of general education has dogged engineering educators every bit as much as how much science and math to incorporate and how to teach engineering. In 1900, the debate focused on social status and prestige, issues that had motivated the shift to classroom learning in the first place. A professional was expected, almost by definition, to be a "gentleman," a term that connoted a well-rounded education. Generally, engineers assumed they could achieve such a distinction through exposure to courses in the liberal arts, but various engineering educators pressed for different classes and subjects in the humanities and social sciences. They argued for the special value of everything from foreign languages to literature, political science to philosophy. Their rationales ranged from a need to smooth the rough edges of engineering students to the value of certain courses for future careers (Baker, 1900; Crandall, 1901; Jackson, 1901; Johnson, 1903; Jones, 1906; Raymond, 1900; Tulleen, 1908).

The discussions focused on three topics, however. First, written communication skills were considered especially important for engineers; hence, engineering schools encouraged the teaching of technical writing, and courses in this area were required for most engineering students (Kynell, 1995; Kynell-Hunt, 1996). Second, nearly all observers felt that engineers needed to understand economics to be better designers and to understand the calculus of profit and loss. In short, they wanted engineers to fit easily into the large corporations that dominate our capitalist society. Third, was history—especially the history of science and engineering. Bridge designer J.A.L. Waddell argued, for example, that engineers needed role models to assume the positions in society they deserved and that historical examples were ideally suited to advancing their professional education. Moreover, the history of past and present accomplishments in technology could teach the general public why engineers deserved to be leaders in society (Fleming, 1920; McDonald, 1921; Pendred, 1923; Prelini, 1920; Waddell, 1903; Zwilgmeyer, 1925).

The list of fields of study that could benefit young engineers was not static. Changing circumstances, as we shall see, led to different emphases at different times. But calls for improving the nontechnical side of engineering education were more or less constant. Every study of engineering education in this century, beginning with the Wickenden report in the 1920s, directed attention to broadening the engineering curriculum.

An especially significant report, *The Aims and Scope of Engineering Education*, was produced by a committee chaired by H.P. Hammond of Penn State. Released in 1940, this study noted that because engineers frequently entered management and assumed duties outside the realm of technical decision making, courses in the liberal arts were clearly important to their success. Hammond coined the term "humanistic stem" to characterize this aspect of engineering education, defining it as parallel to a "scientific-technological stem" of undergraduate course work (Hammond, 1940).

This conceptual scheme guided thinking about the place of nontechnical course work for several decades. During the 1950s, the American Society for Engineering Education received funding from the Ford Foundation and the Carnegie Corporation to review the humanistic stem (Hammond, 1946, 1956). And Case Institute of Technology embarked on a substantial reconstruction of its curriculum designed to produce the best, most broadly educated engineers in the country (Seely, 1995; Shurter, 1952). During the 1960s, Eric Walker's Goals Report strongly emphasized a broad education, and occasional comments about broad education surfaced during the next two decades. Samuel Florman, for example, used the idea as his takeoff point for discussing social responsibility and engineering (Florman, 1976, 1987; Kent, 1978; McCuen, 1983).

But the most telling evidence of continuing attention to nontechnical course work for engineering students can be found in the ABET-sponsored EC 2000 project, which identified 12 competences engineering students need upon graduation. At least half of them, listed as items *a* through *k* under *Criterion 3. Program Outcomes and Assessment*, can be met in large part through courses in social sciences and humanities. These competences include oral and spoken communication, teamwork, understanding of the global and local contexts of engineering, and knowledge of contemporary issues (Caruana, 1999). Discussions about improving and reforming the content of nontechnical engineering education continue, just as they do about scientific and technical education. The discussions today, in fact, deal with the same topics that were current more than a century ago.

SOCIAL INFLUENCES ON ENGINEERING REFORM

Many of the issues to which engineering reformers have devoted significant attention, especially in terms of adjusting curricular content, arose from concerns that were internal to the profession. Put another way, the motivation for reform generally involved issues that engineers themselves felt were important. But as with any group in a larger society, the engineering profession could not determine its shape without taking into account the ideas and expectations of others; indeed, engineering leaders always were sensitive to the opinions of outsiders about engineering.

One of the challenges of engineering, according to historian Edwin Layton, has been the close relationship between engineering and large corporations, the most important outside voice in debates about engineering education. Layton noted that other professions—notably law and medicine—established their professional identities and ethical norms in ways that emphasized their independence from sponsors and employers; both explicitly identified the highest goal as service to society (Layton, 1971). Engineers, however, placed greater emphasis on loyalty and service to employers, arguing that they could best serve society in this way.

It is hardly accidental, then, that engineering educators and employers have always had close ties. Until the 1950s, engineering faculty members, most of whom had practiced engineering before turning to teaching, considered it their goal to train young men for positions in business and industry. William Wickenden, who ran the great study of the 1920s, came to the job from AT&T, and many faculty members spent their summer vacations consulting for industrial firms in order to remain familiar with real-world problems. Large corporations, as historian Thomas Hughes observed, found engineers perfectly suited for the strategic task of incremental research and development (Hughes, 1989). Today, industrial advisory boards to engineering departments, colleges, and universities mark the ongoing ties between industry and engineering education.

Business corporations were not the only outside influence on engineering education. Some engineering education reforms were motivated by events in society at large or by legal or regulatory imperatives. In the former category, we can place the effort to turn engineers into gentlemen who received the rewards of social status and prestige. Respect for expertise was a basic element of the American value system at the turn of the twentieth century, and recognition of engineers' expertise fit nicely into the emergence of a middle class that valued professionalism.

Attitudes and outlooks in American society were never static, however, and as expectations changed, the efforts of engineering educators also changed. Adjustments appeared almost every decade, most often in the humanistic stem. For example, during the 1920s, the wave of technical changes symbolized by Henry Ford's assembly line prompted a significant social interest in efficiency, as well as social acceptance of big business. Engineering schools therefore placed slightly less emphasis on cultural improvement for gentlemen and slightly more emphasis on preparing students for a business environment with accounting and management courses. The economic catastrophe of the Great Depression and talk of technological unemployment, however, undermined some of the enthusiasm for technology and big corporations. As a defensive measure of sorts, engineering curricula placed additional emphasis on economics and other courses that might help explain the Depression (Carey, 1940; Lescohier, 1933; Topping, 1934).

In 1936, at Carnegie Institute of Technology in Pittsburgh, for example, new president Robert E. Doherty responded to the challenges of the Great Depression with the Carnegie Plan, a revamped curriculum that strengthened humanities and social science content. Doherty promised that Carnegie Tech graduates would gain "a clear historical understanding of the parallel growth of science and engineering, on the one hand, and social customs, relations, and institutions, on the other, and of how these have reacted on each other." This social-relations program included a required first-year course entitled "Origins and Development of the Technological Age," which examined the historical development of Western and American civilization, including the role of technology (Boarts and Hodges, 1946; Doherty, 1950a,b).

The logic behind the Carnegie Plan was that students needed to understand and defend the continued development of new technology. But by the late 1930s and continuing into the early 1950s, new problems led to new emphases. World War II and the Cold War encouraged engineering schools to direct students' attention to the nature of government, above all to the differences between democracy and totalitarianism. To inoculate engineering students against the siren song of communism, the humanist stem was significantly strengthened (Green, 1945; Rhys, 1946; Smith, 1945; Wickenden, 1945).

The social activism of the 1960s was felt in engineering schools in several ways. Many engineering schools remained uniquely calm, even hostile, to student antiwar activism; at Michigan Tech, for example, Dow recruiters were received with open arms! But engineering curricula and outlooks did not escape the tumult of the 1960s, although the consequences became visible only over the next two decades.

For example, the environmentalism of Earth Day has become institutionalized in departments of civil and environmental engineering. Indeed, sustainability has become a buzzword among engineering faculty members.

In addition, engineering colleges attempted to recruit more diverse student bodies—especially more women and minority students. The Society for Women Engineers (SWE) had been organized in the late 1940s, just about the time that Cornell's Dean of Engineering Solomon Cady Hollister had commented that women who venture into engineering "must either think and act like men, or they must surrender a considerable amount of their feminine characteristics in the normal pursuance of the professional work" (Alden, 1974; *Cornell Engineer*, 1952; Durchholz, 1977; Hacker, 1983; Oldenziel, 1997; Sproule, 1976). By the 1960s, however, SWE slowly grew into a national organization in the wake of the civil rights and feminist movements. The National Action Council for Minorities in Engineering (NACME) was organized in 1974 (Browne, 1980; *Engineering News-Record*, 1965; Fisher, 1971; Gibbons, 1971; Hartford, 1978; *IEEE Spectrum*, 1975; NACME, 2005).

Although some efforts were made to prepare and recruit racial minorities for engineering careers, neither women nor other minority students are well represented in engineering today. By the late 1990s, however, everyone involved in engineering education—educators and colleges, corporate supporters, and governmental research sponsors—seemed genuinely committed to ensuring that engineering no longer be the most-white, most-male profession.

Diversity is the most obvious way social factors continue to influence efforts to reform engineering education. Such changes are not easy, however. The internal historical logic of engineering seems deeply rooted in a male-oriented past that celebrated virtues such as toughness and strength shown by taming nature for the benefit of society. Such identities die hard.

Although it is now exceedingly rare for women students to encounter faculty members who believe that women should not try to become engineers, Rosalind Williams, a historian of technology and former dean of students at MIT, recently reported that student design teams on her campus position men and women differently. The emerging division of labor suggests that women undertake the "soft" tasks of team building, communication, and contextual preparation and that men do the "real" work of design and innovation (Williams, 2004). Reform, in other words, does not come easy.

REINVENTING THE WHEEL?

Given the difficulty of reform, I use the phrase "reinventing the wheel" to characterize the history of engineering education. I do not mean to say that history repeats itself. Social and political contexts change, and the specific circumstances in which engineering schools, faculties, and students find themselves have changed with new technologies and social developments that pose new challenges. Few engineering deans before 1950 worried much about the relationship between undergraduate and graduate education—or about balancing teaching and research. Fund-raising in its many all-consuming forms looks very different now than it did 25 years ago. And even 10 years ago, few engineering school administrators worried about the outsourcing of U.S. engineering jobs to Asia.

Despite these changes, however, many of the challenges facing engineering educators have remained remarkably consistent over time. The questions of what to include in tight curricula, how long engineering education should last, how much specialization there should be at the undergraduate level, how to prepare students for careers that include both technical and managerial tracks, and how to meet the needs and expectations of society all seem timeless.

As a new round of inquiry and discussions begins, it may be useful to remember that engineering educators have walked this path before and that some of their ideas and solutions might be of value to us. Let me close with a voice from the past—William Wickenden, who headed the 1920s survey of engineering education and later became president of Case Institute of Technology. In 1927, as he was completing that massive study of engineering education in the United States, he wrote, "Closer association between teaching, research, and the working out of original engineering problems would be a potent tonic. What appears to be most needed is an enriched conception of engineering and its place in the social economy, a broader grounding in its principles and methods, and a more general postponement of specialized training to the graduate schools and to the stage of introductory experience which marks the transition to active life" (Wickenden, 1927). Perhaps this prescription still has some efficacy today.

REFERENCES

ABET (Accreditation Board for Engineering and Technology). 2005. Outcome of call for change. Available online at *http://www.abet.org.*

Alden, J.D. 1974. Women and minorities in engineering. Engineering Education 64(7): 498–501.

ASEE (American Society for Engineering Education). 1968. Goals of Engineering Education: Final Report of the Goals Committee. Washington, D.C.: ASEE.

Baker, I.O. 1900. Address by the President. Proceedings of the Society for the Promotion of Engineering Education 8: 11–27.

Boarts, R.M., and J.C. Hodges. 1946. The characteristics of the humanistic-social studies in engineering education: a report. Journal of Engineering Education 36(January): 346.

Browne, L. 1980. The making of minority engineers. Civil Engineering 50(10): 131–134.

Calvert, M. 1967. The Mechanical Engineer in America, 1830–1910: Professional Cultures in Conflict. Baltimore, Md.: Johns Hopkins University Press.

Carey, R.H. 1940. Engineering history and the cultural background. Proceedings of the Society for the Promotion of Engineering Education 30(April): 694–698.

Caruana, C.M. 1999. New accreditation process stirs controversy. Chemical Engineering Progress 95(7): 11–18.

Cornell Engineer. 1952. Where are the women? The Cornell Engineer 18(October): 4.

Cornell University Archives. 1948. Solomon Cady Hollister Papers. Files 40-12, 40-17, and 40-20. Ithaca, N.Y.: Cornell University.

Covert, E.E. 1992. Engineering education in the '90s: back to basics. Aerospace America 30(4): 20–23, 46.

Crandall, C.L. 1901. To what extent should modern languages be required in engineering courses? Proceedings of the Society for the Promotion of Engineering Education 9: 70–75 plus discussion.

Curry, D.T. 1991. Engineering schools under fire. Machine Design 63(20): 10–50.

Derleth, C. 1909. The length of an engineering course. Proceedings of the Society for the Promotion of Engineering Education 17: 134–141.

Dixon, J.R. 1991. New goals for engineering education. Mechanical Engineering 113(3): 56–62.

Doherty, R.E. 1950a. Carnegie Tech, 1936–1950: Review of the Administration of Robert E. Doherty. Pp. 6–12 in file folder 1595, Robert E. Doherty Papers. Pittsburgh, Pa.: Carnegie Mellon University Archives.

Doherty, R.E. 1950b. The Development of Professional Education. Pittsburgh, Pa.: Carnegie Press.

Durchholz, P. 1977. Women in a man's world: the female engineers. Engineering Education 67(January): 292–299.

Engineering News-Record. 1965. Equal opportunity: now a must. Engineering News-Record 175(July 1): 13–14.

Fisher, S. 1971. Minority training programs lurch ahead. Civil Engineering 41(September): 68–72, 75.

Fleming, R. 1920. Needed: a history of engineering. Engineering News-Record 84(February 12): 322–324.

Fletcher, R. 1909. The five and six-year course in engineering schools. Proceedings of the Society for the Promotion of Engineering Education 17: 121–127.

Florman, S.C. 1976. The Existential Pleasures of Engineering. New York: St. Martin's Press.

Florman, S.C. 1987. The Civilized Engineer. New York: St. Martin's Press.

Gibbons, J.F. 1971. A program for education of minority group students in electrical engineering. Proceedings of the IEEE 59(6): 940–945.

Green, R.M. 1945. Need for broad training indicated by University of Nebraska questionnaire. Civil Engineering 15(February): 90–92.

Grinter, L.E. 1956. Report on the evaluation of engineering education. Journal of Engineering Education 46: 25–63.

Hacker, S.L. 1983. Mathematization of Engineering: Limits on Women and the Field. Pp. 38–58 in Machina ex Dea: Feminist Perspectives on Technology, edited by J. Rothschild. New York: Pergamon Press.

Hammond, H.P. 1940. Report of the Committee on Aims and Scope of Engineering Education. Journal of Engineering Education 30: 555–666.

Hammond, H.P. 1946. Report on humanistic social studies in engineering education. Journal of Engineering Education 36(January): 338–351.

Hammond, H.P. 1956. General education in engineering. Journal of Engineering Education 46(April): 619–750.

Hartford, A.F. 1978. Needed: more minority engineers. Chemical Engineering Progress 74(4): 37–39.

Hughes, T.P. 1989. American Genesis: A Century of Invention and Technological Enthusiasm, 1870–1970. New York: Viking Press.

Humphries, A.C. 1913. Four versus five or more years of engineering education. Proceedings of the Society for the Promotion of Engineering Education 21: 322–334.

Hunter, L.C. 1979. A History of Industrial Power in the United States, 1780–1930. Volume 1: Waterpower in the Century of the Steam Engine. Charlottesville, Va.: Eleutherian Mills-Hagley Foundation.

IEEE Spectrum. 1975. EE minorities and discrimination. IEEE Spectrum (September): 72–74.

Jackson, D.C. 1939a. Engineering's Part in the Development of Civilization. New York: American Society of Mechanical Engineers.

Jackson, D.C. 1939b. Present Status and Trends of Engineering Education in the United States. New York: Engineers' Council for Professional Development, Committee on Engineering Schools.

Jackson, J.P. 1901. The arrangement of electrical engineering courses. Proceedings of the Society for the Promotion of Engineering Education 9: 25–40.

Johnson, T.J. 1903. Engineering English. Proceedings of the Society for the Promotion of Engineering Education 11: 361–372.

Jones, B. 1906. Benefit of philosophy to the engineering student. Proceedings of the Society for the Promotion of Engineering Education 14: 97–118.

Kent, J.A. 1978. The role of the humanities and social sciences in technological education. Engineering Education 68(April): 725–734.

Kerr, A.D., and R.B. Pipes. 1987. Why we need hands-on engineering education. Technology Review 90(7): 38.

Kline, R.R. 1984. Origins of the issues [in electrical engineering education]. IEEE Spectrum 21(11): 38–43.

Kline, R.R. 1992. Steinmetz: Engineer and Socialist. Baltimore, Md.: Johns Hopkins University Press.

Kynell, T. 1995. English as an engineering tool: Samuel Chandler Earle and the Tufts experiment. Journal of Technical Writing and Communication 25(1): 85–93.

Kynell-Hunt, T. 1996. Writing in a Milieu of Utility: The Move to Technical Communication in American Engineering Programs, 1850–1950. Norwood, N.J.: Ablex Publishing Corporation.

Landreth, O. 1906. Engineering education. Transactions of the American Society of Civil Engineers 57: 161.

Layton, E.T. 1971. The Revolt of the Engineers: Social Responsibility and the American Engineering Profession. Cleveland, Ohio: Case Western Reserve University Press. Reprinted 1986 by Johns Hopkins University Press, Baltimore, Md.

Lescohier, D.D. 1933. The place of the social sciences in the training of engineers. Proceedings of the Society for the Promotion of Engineering Education 41: 414–421.

Magruder, W.T. 1909. The five-year courses. Proceedings of the Society for the Promotion of Engineering Education 17: 128–133.

Mann, C.R. 1918. Report of the Joint Committee on Engineering Education. Proceedings of the Society for Engineering Education 26: 126–176.

Marburg, E. 1902. Excessive differentiation in engineering courses. Proceedings of the Society for the Promotion of Engineering Education 10: 207–213.

Marvin, F.O. 1901. The cultural value of engineering education. Proceedings of the Society for the Promotion of Engineering Education 9: 13–24.

Masi, C.G. 1995. Re-engineering engineering education. IEEE Spectrum 32(9): 44–47.

McCuen, R.H. 1983. Engineering students' perception of general educational requirements. Journal of Professional Issues in Education 109(4):256–263.

McDonald, P.B. 1921. History of science: a cultural course for engineering students. Engineering and Contracting 56(November 23): 481–482.

MIT Center for Policy Alternatives. 1975. Future Directions for Engineering Education: System Responses to a Changing World. Washington, D.C.: MIT Center for Policy Alternatives.

NACME (National Action Council for Minorities in Engineering). 2005. Nearly 30 years of leadership and support. Available online at http://www.nacme.org.

NRC (National Research Council). 1986. Engineering Undergraduate Education. Washington, D.C.: National Academy Press.

NRC. 1989. Education and Employment of Engineers: A Research Agenda for the 1990s: A Report to the National Academy of Engineering. Issues in Engineering. Washington, D.C.: National Academy Press.

Oldenziel, R. 1997. Decoding the silence: women engineers and male culture in the U.S., 1878–1951. History and Technology 14(3): 1–31.

Pendred, L.St.L. 1923. Value of technological history. Power 58(December 18): 1006.

Prelini, C. 1920. Needed: a history of engineering. Engineering News-Record 84(March 18): 580.

Raymond, W.G. 1900. The promotion of engineering education. Proceedings of the Society for the Promotion of Engineering Education 8: 191–199.

Reynolds, T.S. 1992. The education of engineers in America before the Morrill Act of 1862. History of Education Quarterly 32(4): 459–482.

Reynolds, T.S., and B.E. Seely. 1993. Striving for balance: a hundred years of the American Society for Engineering Education. Journal of Engineering Education 82(July): 136–151.

Rhys, F.W. 1946. Humanistic and social science subjects in relation to the engineering curricula. Proceedings of the Society for the Promotion of Engineering Education 54: 203–206.

Seely, B.E. 1995. SHOT, the history of technology and engineering education. Technology and Culture 36(4): 739–772.

Seely, B.E. 1999. The other re-engineering of engineering education, 1900–1965. Journal of Engineering Education 88(3): 285–294.

Shurter, R.L. 1952. Today's education and tomorrow's engineer. General Electric Review 55 (September): 7-1.

Smith, E.D. 1945. Can humanistic-social study be made engineering education? Journal of Engineering Education 36(October): 134–138.

SPEE (Society for the Promotion of Engineering Education). 1930. Report of the Investigation of Engineering Education, 1923–1929. Vol. 1. Pittsburgh, Pa.: SPEE.

SPEE. 1934. Report of the Investigation of Engineering Education, 1923–1929. Vol. 2. Pittsburgh, Pa.: SPEE.

Sproule, B.A. 1976. Recruiting and keeping women engineering students: an agenda for action. Engineering Education 66(7): 745–747.

Stine, J.K. 1984–1985. Professionalism vs. special interest: the debate over engineering education in nineteenth century America. Potomac Review 26-27: 72–94.

Swain, G.F. 1913. Four versus five or more years of engineering education. Proceedings of the Society for the Promotion of Engineering Education 21: 320–321.

Topping, A.N. 1934. Should our engineering curricula be changed in the light of the present economic situation? Journal of Engineering Education 24(April): 513–518.

Tulleen, J.M. 1908. The courses in English in our technical schools. Proceedings of the Society for the Promotion of Engineering Education 16: 61–74.

Turneaure, F.E. 1909. Tendencies in technical education. Proceedings of the Society for the Promotion of Engineering Education 17: 19–38.

Van Dam, L. 1990. How long should engineering school last? Technology Review 93(October): 12–14.

Waddell, J.A.L. 1903. The advisability of instructing engineering students in the history of the engineering profession. Proceedings of the Society for the Promotion of Engineering Education 11: 193–217.

Walker, E.A. 1989. Now It's My Turn: Engineering My Way. New York: Vantage Press.

Walker, E., and B. Nead. 1966. The Goals Study. Journal of Engineering Education 57(September): 13.

Wickenden, W. 1927. Memo to SPEE Board of Investigation and Coordination, May 14, 1927. Wickenden Committee, Working Papers. Washington, D.C.: American Society of Engineering Education Archives.

Wickenden, W.C. 1945. Goals in engineering education. Electrical Engineering 64(February): 65–68.

Williams, R. 2004. The End of Engineering. Keynote address presented at History of Technology Symposium on the 125th Anniversary of the Ohio Mechanics Institute, University of Cincinnati, March 5, 2004.

Zwilgmeyer, P.G. 1925. History of engineering: a desideratum and an opportunity for A.A.E. Professional Engineer 10(November): 7–9.

Preparation for the Professions Program: Engineering Education in the United States

Sheri Sheppard
Carnegie Foundation for the Advancement of Teaching

The Carnegie Foundation for the Advancement of Teaching has produced many studies of professional education, beginning with the influential Flexner report on medical education in 1910. Building on that tradition, the foundation initiated the Preparation for the Professions Program (PPP) in 1999 to address the perception that professional education has been plagued by a long-standing failure to connect theory and practice in systematic, productive ways. In law schools, for instance, theoretical academic learning is the coin of the realm; little attention is paid to the "lawyering" skills and values that are essential in the world of practice. In addition, professional preparation tends to be insular, with no mechanism for learning from other fields to develop strategies for tackling common challenges of professional preparation. The goal of PPP is to raise issues and broaden the frame of reference for leaders and practitioners in all fields of professional education. Phase I of the program is focused on preparation for three professions—law, the clergy, and engineering. Phase II, simultaneous studies of medical and nursing education, is just being launched.

CONCEPTUAL FRAMEWORK OF THE PROGRAM

During Phase I of the program, the research team developed a framework for addressing topics common to all fields, as well as the particularities of each field. This structure is providing conceptual coherence for the Phase I studies and will be carried forward into Phase II. One concept that is proving useful for comparative purposes, for example, is that each field is characterized by one or more "signature pedagogies," ways of teaching that are familiar, even iconic, to anyone with experience in the field. This concept is based on observations of a ubiquitous pedagogical approach in legal education—so-called Socratic, or case-dialogue, teaching—which has been dramatized in *The Paper Chase* and other films and novels and is thus well known even to the lay public.

The concept of a signature pedagogy has been appropriate to the other fields as well. Each study reveals the nature of the signature pedagogies in that field, suggests their power to encourage a particular kind of learning, identifies their limitations—and suggests creative approaches to overcoming those limitations. Engineering education, for example, is characterized by four very different signature pedagogies, each of them consistent in a particular component of the curriculum (engineering science or "analysis" courses, laboratory courses, design courses, and ethics modules). The three types of courses are thus strikingly different from each other and engender different types of learning. The engineering study takes a close, critical look at each of the signature pedagogies and then considers their relationship to professional roles.

A second lesson from the PPP studies is derived from theoretical efforts to determine the benefits of the old idea of apprenticeship in professional preparation. The idea of "cognitive apprenticeship" is an important aspect of contemporary discussions of how learning occurs (e.g., Brown et al., 1989). To cover the full range of crucial aspects of professional education, we developed a concept of a three-fold apprenticeship:

- **Intellectual training for learning the academic knowledge base and the capacity to think in ways important to the profession.** In engineering, this is generally considered the main goal of analysis classes, in which the emphasis is on understanding fundamental concepts.
- **A skill-based apprenticeship of practice**, which is the focus in engineering laboratory and design settings. In these situations, faculty act primarily as advisors, consultants, and coaches to student teams working on projects.
- **An apprenticeship in the mission, ethical standards, social**

roles, and responsibilities of the profession, through which the integrated practice of all dimensions of the profession and the fundamental purposes of the profession are introduced. This apprenticeship may be integrated into laboratory or design settings, taught in stand-alone classes, or not taught explicitly at all.

These aspects of professional apprenticeship reflect different emphases in all professional education and are deeply rooted in the history and organization of professional schools. By examining these apprenticeships, we can characterize common issues across fields, as well as distinct issues in each field. The metaphor of a three-fold apprenticeship also forms a basis for a normative analysis, a lens through which to evaluate the adequacy of preparation for professional work. Based on this framework, the study team was able to describe the tensions and shortfalls, as well as the strengths, of professional education in each field.

Assessment of student learning has emerged as a salient area in each field we investigated so far and is closely linked to the pedagogical theme of basic practices of teaching and learning. Assessment that helps students both master subject matter and become more aware of their capacities can be a key contributor in professional education to the formation of competent practitioners. Assessment includes ongoing informal feedback on performance, as well as formal assessments. Despite its importance, however, assessment is a troublesome issue in all three of the fields in Phase I and is emerging as a central concern for the professions in the Phase II studies. Coaching and continuous, informative feedback are critical to an effective apprenticeship, so assessment practices give specific content to aspects of the apprenticeship framework and provide a basis for making comparisons across fields.

THE STUDY OF ENGINEERING EDUCATION

In the first stage of the engineering study (2000–2001), we took a "big picture" approach to answering questions about teaching and learning practices in engineering education in the United States. We reviewed data from a national survey and ABET self-studies from 40 engineering schools (100 programs) to select seven schools to look at in greater detail through site visits. The selected schools are located in all regions of the United States and include a wide range of institutional types—a small stand-alone school of engineering, a large public engineering school, several university-based programs, a Catholic university, and a school that serves many first-generation college students and transfer students. Thus, striking similarities and important variations among the schools are described. The study team visited these schools during the first six months of 2002, interviewing more than 200 faculty and 200 students and administrators and observing 60 classes.

An important goal of the data analysis has been to develop a clear picture of how administrators, faculty, and students understand the nature of engineering practice and to identify a set of core ideas that are consistent across these groups and in line with published analyses of the essential features of the profession. The resulting conception of what an engineer is and what an engineer does is laid out in the first chapter and provides a "backbone" for the book. In subsequent chapters, curricula and pedagogies are described in some detail and then examined with reference to how well they contribute to preparation for the practice of engineering. Draft chapters addressing the three main components of the curriculum—analysis, laboratory, and design courses—are finished, as are detailed outlines of the other chapters. A draft of the full manuscript should be completed by the summer of 2005.

REFERENCE

Brown, J.S., A. Collins, and S.E. Newman. 1989. Cognitive apprenticeship: teaching the crafts of reading, writing, and mathematics. In L.B. Resnick (Ed.), *Knowing, Learning, and Instruction: Essays in Honor of Robert Glaser* (pp. 453-494). Hillsdale, N.J.: Lawrence Erlbaum Associates.

International Recognition of Engineering Degrees, Programs, and Accreditation Systems

Kevin Sweeney
Miami University

As economic globalization increases, we must bring down artificial barriers that limit workforce mobility. One way to increase mobility is through the mutual recognition of degrees, degree programs, and accreditation systems. Some places—Europe, for example—have a strong desire to work towards global harmonization, and, given the expansion of the European Union (EU) and its need for workforce mobility, regional harmonization as well. This has provoked a great deal of activity, especially in countries that do not have recognized accreditation systems in place, or even a tradition of accreditation, such as Germany. The United States, which has a strong tradition of engineering accreditation, is also working toward global recognition of accreditation methods. Mutual recognition and accreditation will not only benefit graduates in a particular country, but will also promote quality control and attract students to national degree programs.

It is generally accepted that a competent practicing engineer must have the following qualifications:

- a strong education that teaches analytical and theoretical thinking that enables problem solving, innovation, and invention
- training in working with people from diverse backgrounds and solving technical problems
- work experience, including responsibility for making decisions

As Jack Levy (EUR ING Professor at the City University in the United Kingdom) has said (2002), "While these components of competence of professionalism are needed, the *way* they are acquired varies, as does the point at which the national professional title is awarded . . . [and] the length of the academic course may vary widely, from three years to five or more years."

In the following sections, current activities dealing with mutual recognition of accreditation of engineering degree programs, engineering technologist degree programs, and the professional level for registered engineering practitioners are summarized.

ENGINEERING DEGREE PROGRAMS

Washington Accord

The Washington Accord was signed in 1989 by the groups in Australia, Canada, Ireland, New Zealand, the United Kingdom, and the United States responsible for accrediting professional engineering degree programs in their countries. The accord recognizes "substantial equivalency" of the programs accredited by the signatories and satisfaction of the "academic requirements for the practice of engineering at the professional level." The accord states that the "processes, policies and procedures" used in the accreditation of academic programs are comparable and "recommends that graduates of accredited programs in any of the signatory countries be recognized by the other countries as having met the academic requirements for entry to the practice of engineering" (Washington Accord, 2004).

The Washington Accord has several limitations. First, it covers professional engineering undergraduate programs but not engineering technology or postgraduate programs. Second, it does not apply to degree programs accredited before signing by the accrediting body. Third, it does not apply to degree programs declared or recognized as "substantially equivalent" by the signatories. Finally, it covers only the academic requirements of licensing, but not the actual licensing, which still varies from country to country.

Interest in the Washington Accord has increased significantly since it was signed in 1989. Two more countries have signed on since then and are now full signatories: Hong Kong in 1995 and South Africa in

1999. Four countries have been added as provisional signatories: Japan in 2001 and Germany, Malaysia, and Singapore in 2003. In addition, the accreditation bodies of India and Bangladesh have recently expressed their intent to submit applications for provisional membership, and Russia and Korea have sent representatives to meetings of the Washington Accord signatories.

Alec Hay, chairman of the International Committee of the Engineering Council of South Africa, stated while reporting on a June 2001 meeting on the Washington Accord that "Being a signatory to the WA [Washington Accord] remains therefore a significant development for South Africa and is in line with the Government's perspective that the standards in engineering should meet international standards."

A recent paper by Professor M.K. Khanijo (2004), senior consultant with the Engineering Council of India, describes India's motivation for signing on to the Washington Accord: "Since GATS [General Agreement of Trade in Services] emphasizes recognition of qualifications of professionals, it is in India's interest to get its own system of recognition and registration made acceptable at the international level. If this is not done, Indian engineers will be at a disadvantage and may even be ruled out when they seek opportunities for employment."

Although membership in the Washington Accord is considered by many national accreditation agencies as the best path towards international recognition, some concerns remain about whether developing nations can be accepted as full members.

The EUR ING Professional Title

The Fédération Européenne d'Associations Nationales d'Ingénieurs (FEANI) (translated as the European Federation of National Engineering Associations) is a federation of national engineering associations from the EU, European Free Trade Association, and countries considered "eligible for accession into the EU" at a future time. Currently, FEANI, which has 26 member countries representing more than two million professional engineers, considers itself "the single voice for the engineering profession in Europe" and is working to "affirm and develop the professional identity of engineers." The European Commission recognizes FEANI as the official representative of the engineering profession in Europe (FEANI, 2005).

One of the services provided by FEANI, the granting of the EUR ING professional title, is intended to "facilitate the mutual recognition of engineering qualifications in Europe" and (1) facilitate mobility by assigning a "guarantee of competence" to engineers who wish to practice outside their own countries, (2) provide information to employers about educational and training systems in Europe, and (3) encourage continuous improvements in the quality of engineers by monitoring and reviewing standards. Currently, slightly fewer than 30,000 registered engineers have been granted the EUR ING title.

FEANI maintains an index of universities and other institutions of higher education and their engineering degree programs recognized as fulfilling the mandatory educational requirements for the EUR ING title. Member countries submit descriptions of schools and degree programs for inclusion in the FEANI Index upon approval by the European Monitoring Committee. The FEANI Index is intended to be the "authoritative source of information about national engineering education systems and educational institutions" (FEANI, 2000).

Other Pan-European Organizations

The European Standing Observatory for the Engineering Profession and Education (ESOEPE), which is associated with FEANI, comprises organizations concerned "with quality assurance and accreditation of engineering programmes, including national and trans-national (European) bodies, Associations or temporary networks." ESOEPE has aspirations of becoming *the* European body dealing with accreditation (FEANI, 2001). In fact, ESOEPE has considered changing its name to the European Consortium for Engineering Accreditation.

The European Parliament is currently considering a directive [COM(2004)317] that would accelerate the processing of requests for recognition of qualifications by giving more automatic recognition to engineers who meet certain agreed criteria. The purpose would be to bridge differences in education and training and make it easier for engineers and other professionals to work anywhere in the EU.

Many other pan-European organizations are addressing the issue of mutual recognition of accreditation and quality control in higher education. Currently, there is a good deal of discussion, even competition, about which models for European-wide accreditation of degrees will prevail and which organizations will take the lead. Some of these organizations are listed below:

- The European Consortium for Accreditation in Higher Education (ECA) was established in 2003 to achieve "mutual recognition of accreditation decisions among the participants before the end of 2007" (ECA, 2003).
- The European Network for Quality Assurance in Higher Education (ENQA) was "established to promote European co-operation in the field of quality assessment and quality assurance between all actors involved in the quality assurance process" (ENQA, 2000).
- The Network of Central and Eastern European Quality Assurance Agencies in Higher Education (CEE Network), founded in 2001, was established "to serve as a clearinghouse for issues on quality assurance in higher education in the Central and Eastern European countries" (CEE Network, 2001).
- The Joint Quality Initiative, "an informal network for quality assurance and accreditation of bachelor and master programmes in Europe," is based on the Bologna Declaration of 1999 and the Prague Communiqué of 2001. The Joint Quality Initiative works to "adopt a higher education system essentially based on two main cycles, to co-operate in quality assurance, to design scenarios for mutual acceptance of evaluation and accreditation/certification mechanisms, to collaborate in establishing a common framework of reference, and to disseminate best practice" (Joint Quality Initiative, 2000).
- The European Network of Information Centers (ENIC Network) was formed "to develop policy and practice for the recognition of qualifications" and to provide information on the recognition of foreign diplomas, degrees, and other qualifications; educational systems throughout Europe; and opportunities for studying abroad, including information on loans and scholarships and answers to practical questions related to mobility and equivalence (ENIC, 1999).
- The National Academic Recognition Information Centers Network (NARIC Network) was initiated by the European Commission in 1984 to improve academic recognition of diplomas

and periods of study in EU member states, EEA countries, and associated countries in Central and Eastern Europe and Cyprus (NARIC, 1984).

ENGINEERING AND TECHNOLOGY DIPLOMA/DEGREE PROGRAMS

Sydney Accord

Signed in 2001, the Sydney Accord, which provides for joint recognition of academic programs for engineering technologists, is based on the Washington Accord and operates in a similar way. Current members include the national engineering organizations of Ireland, the United Kingdom, Canada, South Africa, Hong Kong, Australia, and New Zealand.

Dublin Accord

Signed in 2002, the Dublin Accord, which provides joint recognition of academic programs for engineering technicians, is also based on the Washington Accord and operates in a similar way. Representatives of the national engineering organizations of the United Kingdom, South Africa, Canada, and Ireland have all signed on to this agreement (Dublin Accord, 2002).

THE PROFESSIONAL LEVEL OF REGISTERED PRACTITIONERS

Engineers Mobility Forum

The Engineers Mobility Forum (EMF), established in October 1997, was initially formed as a subcommittee of the Washington Accord signatories to facilitate the mobility of experienced professional engineers. Unlike the Washington Accord, which focuses on mutual recognition of accredited academic programs, EMF is developing "a system of mutual recognition of the full professional level to facilitate cross-border mobility of registered practitioners." This is especially important for currently practicing engineers whose qualifications are not recognized through the Washington Accord (EMF, 2003).

EMF maintains a decentralized Register of International Engineers that includes the names of professional engineers in member countries who meet very specific educational and experiential guidelines. The purpose of the registry is to streamline the process of obtaining practice privileges in EMF-member countries. The registry is "decentralized" in the sense that each country operates its own section and writes its own "assessment statement" describing the admission requirements for that country. A monitoring committee in each country develops the assessment statement, reviews applications for admission to the registry, and functions as the point of contact for all matters relating to the registry.

EMF members include the national engineering organizations of Ireland, the United Kingdom, United States, Canada, South Africa, Hong Kong, Australia, Japan, Malaysia, Korea, and New Zealand. FEANI has observer status, and India and Bangladesh have expressed an interest in joining EMF.

With the signing of the EMF Agreement in June 2001, the International Register of Professional Engineers (IRoPE) was established (IPENZ, 2000). The requirements for entrants to the registry are listed below (BCS, 2005):

- registration in a signatory jurisdiction
- accredited degree or equivalent academic qualification
- seven years postgraduate experience
- two years of work with responsibility for engineering work
- maintenance of continuing professional development

Asia-Pacific Economic Cooperation Engineer Register

Similar to IRoPE, the Asia-Pacific Economic Cooperation (APEC) Engineer Register is an initiative that facilitates cross-border mobility for professional engineers in the APEC region. An APEC Engineer Register has been established in Australia, Canada, Hong Kong China, Indonesia, Japan, Korea, Malaysia, New Zealand, the Philippines, Thailand, and the United States.

In the United States, the EMF and APEC registers are maintained by the U.S. Council for International Engineering Practice (USCIEP), which was established to "develop and promote procedures to enable U.S.-registered professional engineers to practice internationally" (USCIEP, 2004). Member organizations of USCIEP include the

Accreditation Board for Engineering and Technology (ABET), the National Council of Examiners for Engineering and Surveying, the National Society of Professional Engineers, and the Association of Consulting Engineers of Canada.

Requirements for admission to the USCIEP Registry include licensing in one or more jurisdictions of the United States and the qualifications listed below:

- graduation from an accredited program (either via ABET or the Washington Accord)
- a passing grade on the Fundamentals of Engineering examination
- a passing grade on one or more of the Principles and Practice of Engineering assessment examinations
- no sanctions resulting in a suspension or revocation by any jurisdiction of the engineering practice license
- at least five references from licensed professional engineers familiar with the candidate's work, character, and integrity
- periodic updates of the professional activities record and testimonials from professional references
- at least seven years of qualifying experience (at least four at the time of initial registration as a professional engineer)
- at least two years of experience in charge of significant engineering work as defined in the USCIEP Assessment Statement
- minimum standards for continuing professional competence as a condition of remaining on the registry as defined in the USCIEP Assessment Statement
- citizenship in the United States

Engineering Technologists Mobility Forum

Similar to the EMF, the Engineering Technologists Mobility Forum (ETMF) was established to remove "artificial barriers to the free movement and practice of certified/registered/licensed engineering technologists amongst their jurisdictions." The agreement specifically covers the process by which substantial equivalence in competence of practitioners is established. Signatories of ETMF include Canada, Ireland, New Zealand, South Africa, and the United Kingdom (IPENZ, 2004).

Other Agreements

Many bilateral and multilateral agreements have been established between countries and organizations. Although these agreements may still be important, especially on a regional level, they are rapidly being preempted by large-scale, multinational, mutual agreements.

REFERENCES

BCS (British Computer Society). 2005. International Register of Professional Engineers: Entry Criteria. Available online at *http://www.bcs.org/BCS/MembersArea/ InternationalEng/EntryCriteria.htm.*

CEE Network (Network of Central and Eastern European Quality Assurance Agencies in Higher Education). 2001. About the CEE Network. Available online at *http:// www.ceenetwork.hu/a_about.html.*

Dublin Accord. 2002. The Dublin Accord, Recognition of Equivalence of Educational Base for Engineering Technicians. Available online at *http://www.ecsa.co.za/International/ 6DublinAccord/Dublin%20Accord%20Agreement%2013May2002.pdf.*

ECA (European Consortium for Accreditation in Higher Education). 2003. About ECA. Available online at *http://www.ecaconsortium.net.*

EMF (Engineers Mobility Forum). 2003. A Review of Recognition Systems for Professional Engineers. In Global Challenges in Engineering Education: Proceedings of the 2003 ASEE/WFEO International Colloquium on Engineering Education. Washington, D.C.: American Society for Engineering Education. Also available online at *http:// www.asee.org/about/events/conferences/international/papers/upload/A-Review-of-Recognition-Systems.pdf.*

ENIC (European Network of Information Centers). 1999. The European Gateway to Recognition of Academic and Professional Qualifications. Available online at *http:// www.enic-naric.net.*

ENQA (European Network for Quality Assurance in Higher Education). 2000. About ENQA. Available online at *http://www.enqa.net.*

FEANI (Fédération Européenne d'Associations Nationales d'Ingénieurs). 2000. FEANI Index. Available online at *http://www.feani.org/FEANIindex.htm.*

FEANI. 2001. European Standing Observatory for the Engineering Profession and Education (ESOEPE). Available online at *http://www.feani.org/ESOEPE/Bye-lawsFIN.htm.*

FEANI. 2005. FEANI—The Voice of Europe's Engineers. Available online at *http:// www.feani.org.*

Hay, A.J. 2001. International Affairs Consolidated Report: Meetings of the Washington Accord, Sydney Accord, Engineers Mobility Forum and Engineering Technologists' Mobility Forum, Thornybush Game Reserve, June 20–26, 2001, South Africa. Available online at *http://www.ecsa.co.za.*

IPENZ (Institution of Professional Engineers New Zealand). 2000. Engineers Mobility Forum Agreement: To Establish and Maintain an EMF International Register of Professional Engineers. Final draft. Available online at *http://www.ipenz.org.nz/ipenz/forms/ pdfs/EMF_Agreement.pdf.*

IPENZ. 2004. Engineering Technologists Mobility Forum, MOU, Signed June 2001 at Thornybush Game Reserve, South Africa. Available online at *http://www.ipenz.org.nz/ ipenz/finding/etmf/MOU.cfm.*

Joint Quality Initiative. 2000. Joint Quality Initiative Website Welcome. Available online at *http://www.jointquality.org.*

Khanijo, M.K. 2004. Implications of GATS on the engineering profession. Available online at *http://www.iete.info/ECI/ImplicationsGATS.htm.*

Levy, J. 2002. International Recognition of Engineering Qualifications. In The Renaissance Engineer of Tomorrow: Proceedings of the 30th SEFI Annual Conference. Brussels, Belgium: European Society for Engineering Education (SEFI).

NARIC (National Academic Recognition Information Centers Network). 1984. The European Gateway to Recognition of Academic and Professional Qualifications. Available online at *http://www.enic-naric.net.*

USCIEP (U.S. Council for International Engineering Practice). 2004. What Is USCIEP? Available online at *http://www.usciep.org/what_is.shtml.*

Washington Accord. 2004. Frequently Asked Questions. Available online at *http:// www.washingtonaccord.org/wash_accord_faq.html.*

Appendix B

These transcripts of presentations given at the plenary sessions of the 2004 Engineering Education Summit served as catalysts for the discussions that occurred in the breakout groups. They represent the opinions of the individual speakers and are not necessarily endorsed by the Engineer of 2020 Phase II Committee. The Committee wishes to express its thanks to all of the speakers for their contribution to the Summit.

Capturing the Imagination: High-Priority Reforms for Engineering Educators

Gretchen Kalonji
University of Washington

My remarks are based on lessons learned in recent years, particularly through the National Science Foundation (NSF) Engineering Education Coalitions, but also through other notable efforts to reform science education at both the university and K-12 levels. A great many projects have been undertaken, and we have accumulated quite a bit of data about what works well and what doesn't. There have been many successful innovations that can help us in planning for the future: the benefits of interdisciplinary, team-based design activities early in the curriculum; the power of novel linkages with K-12 programs and student leadership activities; the importance of the innovative integration of technology (particularly when students are involved in its design and implementation); the importance of alternative approaches to assessing student learning; the need for programs for graduate student and faculty development; and the implications of all of these for diversity in our communities.

Even if we could scale up what works in the intellectual and professional development of students and in increasing diversity in the engineering workforce, we would still not be able to address the problems we face nationally in engineering education. That is because most of the work up to now has been performed in the framework of perceived and/or real constraints, focused mostly on the curriculum, particularly the transformation of courses creatively about the kind of activities that promote the intellectual and professional development of students, we have fallen back on old educational metaphors. To a certain extent, both students and faculty are burdened by the tyranny of the assumption that "courses" are the primary (and in many cases almost the sole) mechanisms for student intellectual development.

As we move forward, we must boldly reformulate engineering education. To put it bluntly, by sticking to existing models, we are losing the battle for the imaginations of young people. Many of the best, most creative, most idealistic, and most energetic young people do not see a future for themselves in engineering that engages their passions. Instead, many see engineering education as a formulaic, boring, individualistic endeavor driven largely by the acquisition of highly atomized, esoteric technical skills. The connection in students' minds between engineering and the issues they care about is obscure. Even those who recognize engineering as a venue for solving major problems facing humanity often become discouraged in the early years by the seemingly endless drudgery of courses that appear to be largely disconnected, not only from their interests, but also from the broader picture of what engineering could be, and should be, about.

Besides losing the battle for the imaginations of young people, we are not addressing the rapidly changing nature of professional practice. Considering the rapid pace of change and the internationalization of technical labor, there simply will not be jobs for our students unless we begin to think more creatively about the kinds of skills and personal development they will need to be competitive.

I am arguing for a dramatic, fundamental transformation of the educational process. Instead of an education based on courses, we should focus on participation in multidisciplinary, multisectoral, multicultural, even multinational teams addressing the grand challenges facing our world. Let engineering capture the intellectual high ground of transforming higher education across disciplines by challenging the fundamental structure of undergraduate education. In this reformulation, the heart of the curriculum is participation—in interdisciplinary teams and in substantive research projects. This new approach might be called a "grand challenges curriculum."

Examples of grand challenges could include: the development of effective, low-cost wastewater treatment technologies to make clean water accessible to more people around the world; new health care diagnostic technologies; the transformation of decaying urban infrastructures; and so on. Because the lines between science and technology are being increasingly blurred (e.g., nanotechnology and bioengineering), basic challenges at the frontiers of science should also be included. Superb science also serves humanity.

Building a curriculum around grand challenges would mean that courses as we currently think of them would have a subsidiary, supporting role. The predominant activities of students would change dramatically, as would the role of faculty. In structuring this new educational paradigm, we can learn from the NSF Engineering Education Coalitions and other projects:

- Engage students in exciting, team-based, *authentic* experiences in their freshmen year. We can build here on the experience of the NSF Engineering Education Coalitions.

- Help students develop *intellectual road maps of their field(s)* (a moving target for many). The road maps should include "milestones," that is, specific knowledge and skills they will need and why. Some of these milestones may be reachable through existing courses, but we should be open to defining alternative mechanisms and alternative ways of certifying these skills.

- Provide students with *multiple entry points and exit points*. We must preserve the extraordinary flexibility of the U.S. higher education system and encourage students to explore a variety of interests without inordinate penalties. Even a student who starts and finishes her degree in one institution would benefit greatly from "messing around" a bit and working on a number of challenges before zeroing in on an area of specialization.

- Establish *interdisciplinary working teams* to address challenges thatinclude, as appropriate, faculty and students from social sciences and humanities, natural sciences, business and law, and other disciplines. Of course, if the challenges are big enough, the research will have to be interdisciplinary. This would also give students who initially thought engineering was boring a chance to take a second look and maybe reconsider. Interdisciplinary teams can also further diversity.

- Offer students multiple *opportunities for leadership*, either in the K-12 community, in the design and delivery of educational technology, or in service projects to local communities. Students are our most underutilized resource in making educational change.

- Promote *extra-university partnerships*. The new educational metaphor will require more involvement with state and local government, the nonprofit sector and industry. These deeper and broader multisector partnerships will have a number of ancillary benefits for students.
- Develop *international alliances* to enhance partnerships. Benefits include: preparing students educationally and professionally for the world arena in which they will be working and the transnational dimensions of the challenges they will face; overcoming the insularity of the U.S. engineering education community; and increasing the diversity of the student body. Women, for example, are significantly overrepresented in most "study abroad" programs. If we choose partners and topics carefully (e.g., working closely with partner universities around the world), internationalizing student projects can be a strategy for increasing ethnic and cultural diversity.
- Continue (albeit with some modifications) *the culminating senior thesis/design project, either as an individual or as part of a team.* Students must have the experience of completing and presenting a substantive body of work before they move to the next stage of their lives.

An undergraduate engineering education based on participation in multidisciplinary teams working on major, or grand, challenges will have a variety of ancillary benefits. Students will develop strong leadership, communication, and teamwork skills, cross-cultural and cross-national awareness, and most important, confidence in their ability to contribute to the science and engineering community.

In the new educational setting, faculty will experience the intellectual excitement of learning new things and building new partnerships and will be able to focus more energy on the things they really care about, such as contributing to important research, making a real difference in young people's lives, and contributing to society. The emotional rewards for faculty are a key element in a transformed educational environment.

If the new educational environment is carefully constructed, it can also benefit institution in many ways: by increasing the credibility of the institution with stakeholders as university research is targeted toward solving local societal problems; by establishing better partnerships with local organizations and international allies; and by making institutions more attractive to students and faculty from diverse backgrounds.

The engineering profession will be more likely to capture the imaginations of young people, thus moving engineering to the forefront as educational institutions rethink and redesign undergraduate education. Engineering graduates will be among the most creative, energetic, and dynamic young professionals in the world.

CONCLUSION

In this brief summary, I have outlined where I think engineering education should be going and some of the steps we must take to move from a curriculum focused on courses to a curriculum focused on collaborative, interdisciplinary projects. Individual institutions can do a lot; multi-institutional alliances can do much more. Catalyzing the results of experiments in the pragmatics of educational transformation would be very useful. For the health of the system as a whole, we should maintain institutional diversity in "flavors" and approaches.

The University of Washington has taken some steps in the direction I have described. Through an initiative I led called UW Worldwide, the university is bringing together faculty and students not just in engineering, but also from a wide variety of other colleges and schools, to work with partner universities around the world on multinational, project-based education. Our flagship project is a joint, four-year, research-based undergraduate curriculum with Sichuan University focusing on challenges to the environment in the U.S. Pacific Northwest and southwest China. This program combines research in water quality and wastewater treatment, eco-materials, forest ecology, and biodiversity with extensive language and cultural studies and a reciprocal year-long exchange. This is just a beginning, though. Our hope is that this initiative will be a model for networks of projects and institutions working together to transform the curriculum to focus on participation in large-scale, team-based research challenges.

The Global Engineer

Linda Katehi
Purdue University

As I was preparing for this panel, I read *The Engineer of 2020* with great interest (NAE, 2004). One particular section attracted my attention. It describes scenarios for the future, four alternative environments, all futuristic, each one taking us in a different direction. When I finished reading, I was thankful that none of them was real and intrigued by a future so wonderfully unknown. And yet, the unknown that makes the future beautiful and wonderful in the eyes of some, also makes us vulnerable. This vulnerability has become clear in the present economic environment.

In the last few years, the U.S. engineering workforce has undergone trends that we would never have anticipated 10 or 20 years ago—the outsourcing of mainstream engineering jobs; increasing reliance on foreign-born Ph.D. graduates; and the need for retraining engineers to enable them to change careers a number of times before retirement.

As we try to predict the future of the engineering profession and engineering education, we must take into account some important factors. First, history has shown that changes in the engineering profession follow changes in cultural, social, and political environments. Evidence shows that these changes in the profession have led to technology breakthroughs that helped or harmed social progress, depending on the political environment surrounding them.

Second, as we think about the engineering profession of the future and education to prepare the engineer of 2020 and beyond, we should keep in mind statistical projections relevant to anticipated social and economic changes:

- By 2050, 8 billion of the 9 billion people on Earth will live in developing countries, and economic growth in these countries will be only 2 percent below the expected economic growth in the developed world.
- In 20 to 30 years, the most popular language will not be English, and what we now consider U.S. industries will not exist in their present form. If these industries exist by name at all, their headquarters will not be in the United States.
- By 2050, the biggest social problem occupying the world will be poverty, and its primary impact will be on the female population.
- In 20 to 30 years, the primary economic growth in nations around the world will depend on females working in all professions, from farming to high-tech industry.

THE U.S. ENGINEER OF 2020 AND BEYOND

With these factors in mind, it is very easy to conclude that U.S. engineers will face totally different problems from the ones we face today. It is expected that U.S. engineers will be based abroad, will have to travel (physically or virtually) around the world to meet customers, and will have to converse proficiently in more than one language. U.S. engineers will represent a minority culture and, thus, will have to be open to different religions, different ways of thinking, and different social values. Flexibility and respect for ways of life different from ours will be critical to professional success.

Future U.S. engineers will have to address and help solve a variety of problems, from creating means of communication among indigenous groups to reducing or eliminating poverty to providing transportation to addressing environmental problems to accommodating new technology breakthroughs in solutions to becoming accustomed to a technology progress rate 10 to 100 times faster than today's rate.

U.S. engineers must become global engineers. They will have to know how to replenish their knowledge by self-motivated, self-initiated learning. They will have to be aware of socioeconomic changes and appreciate the impact of these changes on the social and economic landscape in the United States and elsewhere. The engineer of 2020 and beyond will need skills to be globally competitive over the length of her or his career.

ENGINEERING EDUCATION

History has shown that the "Great American Engineering College" has been extremely conservative in terms of curricular issues. This indigenous and historical conservatism has been compounded by the over-specification and over-prescription of educational requirements. However, revising the curriculum has become a heroic and very expensive task. As a result, university curricula structures last for long periods of time, sometimes more than 20 years.

When it comes to changes in the curriculum, we tend to focus on the successes of the past rather than the challenges of the future. As *The Engineer of 2020* states, "we are teaching more and more about less and less." As our interest and awareness of global problems increases, our teaching efforts are increasingly being perceived as pointless attempts to teach everything about nothing.

Although the future is unpredictable, the skills required for engineers to be successful are well known. And one thing is for sure—the future will be global. Neither the United States nor any other developed country will be able to ignore global issues. Addressing poverty and health care delivery on a global scale and accepting social responsibility will not be matters of philanthropy but of survival.

Current Challenges

Engineering schools today are facing a challenge they have never faced before. They must prepare engineers for solving unknown problems and not for addressing assumed scenarios. Therefore, the emphasis should be on teaching to learn rather than providing more knowledge. Teaching engineers to think analytically will be more important than helping them memorize algebra theorems. Teaching them to cope with rapid progress will be more critical than teaching them all of the technology breakthroughs.

We have seen in the past 20 years that the amount of new knowledge increases at a logarithmic rate in all technology and physical science disciplines. It is fascinating that all of this information is available at the click of a keyboard key.

Future Learning Paradigms

The new engineering curriculum must take into account that in the future students will learn in a completely different way. Up to now, engineering schools have developed curricula by creating scenarios or predicting the problems we expect to face. In doing so, we have focused on knowledge rather than skills.

Curricula based on specific knowledge are built from the bottom up. In this teaching paradigm, we dissect a hypothetical problem into a myriad of pieces. We then teach about each of these pieces, anticipating that we will be able to develop a solution by combining them. As the complexity of the problem increases, however, the relative size of the building blocks becomes smaller. Eventually, the effort involved in learning about the small pieces is so overwhelming that we can no longer synthesize the original problem—the parts become more important than the whole. Engineers whose education is built from the bottom up cannot comprehend and address big problems. They get lost in irrelevant details.

Solving Unknown Problems

In a scenario-free future, there are no anticipated problems, only anticipated challenges and possible opportunities. The future engineering curriculum should be built around developing skills and not around teaching available knowledge. We must focus on shaping analytic skills, problem-solving skills, and design skills. We must teach methods and not solutions. We must teach future engineers to be creative and flexible, to be curious and imaginative.

Future engineers must understand and appreciate the impact of social/cultural dynamics on a team environment. They must appreciate the power of a team relative to the importance of each individual's talent. They must know how to communicate effectively and how to think globally. Engineering curricula must focus on developing skills that enable them to address the unknown.

CREATING GLOBAL ENGINEERS

We need engineering curricula that are not overly prescribed, that focus on how to learn and how to apply what has been learned. We need to focus on how to seek and find information. We need curricula that satisfy a few fundamental teaching principles but allow for true variations. Requirements must be flexible to react to change. Future engineers will need design skills, as well as analytical skills.

We must also open engineering curricula to non-engineers and teach our students how to solve social problems and how to commoditize technical innovations and processes to erase poverty. We must recreate connections between engineering and the larger society and focus on tools that will improve the quality of life. American engineering schools are facing a great challenge, and we should be looking forward to making it an opportunity for national and global leadership.

REFERENCE

NAE (National Academy of Engineering). 2004. *The Engineer of 2020: Visions of Engineering in the New Century.* Washington, D.C.: The National Academies Press.

The Importance of Economics

G. Bennett Stewart, III
Stern Stewart & Co.

Given my slim curriculum vitae and engineering credentials, I agreed to speak only on the condition that Princeton Professor John Mulvey not revoke my engineering degree. This is the first lesson of risk management, of which Mulvey is a world expert. I should explain that I entered Princeton's engineering program in 1970 because my father was an engineer, I was good at math and science, and I enjoyed solving problems. But like many, many others, I didn't know what to expect, and by the end of my freshman year, in 1971, I didn't know which of the five departments to choose. A fellow engineer and roommate, Larry McKeithan, helped. "Bennett," he said, "it's electrical engineering. Computers are the wave of the future." That was enough to convince me. At the end of my junior year, when I was once again approaching a fork in the road, I consulted my *consigliere* Larry again. "Business school," he advised. "What's that?" I asked. "I'm not sure," he said, "but it gets you a job at the end."

With the next stage of my education carefully plotted, off I went to the University of Chicago, which at the time was an engineer's delight. Finance was taught like a branch of physics—mathematical models and empirical research into stock market and accounting data, and, in my humble opinion, the world's best economics department. I lapped it up, while, to my satisfaction, undergraduate liberal arts majors struggled mightily.

The Chicago business education is now decidedly different than it was in my time. It now includes more case studies, more teamwork, more of the "real world," largely in reaction to popular rankings published in *Business Week* magazine and other publications. Based on my experience interviewing Chicago students, recent graduates are more verbal, less one-dimensional, "slicker" than we were, but also less substantive. In exchange for more immediate market value, they appear to have surrendered foundations and skills I believe are of lifelong value. Although they may be better at addressing questions of the moment, I suspect they lack the ability to adapt readily to unpredictable changes, and therein may lie a lesson for the education of engineers.

To complete this short story, I ended up joining the corporate financial advisory arm of the Chase Manhattan Bank, from which, in 1982, a group of us left to start our own management consulting firm specializing in valuation, financial management, and incentive compensation. And in this work I have found my training as an engineer to be of real value, not so much in specific ways, although there certainly were specifics, particularly in the early years, but in the rational, systemic, problem-solving mind-set engineering education fosters. That is a gift I have cherished, and I owe it to the outstanding and dedicated engineering faculty at Princeton. I have been fortunate, and will not forget it.

And that brings me at long last to my first pertinent comment, based on my particular set of experiences. Engineers must learn economics. Not high-faluting Keynesian macroeconomics, but basic micro-economics, the setting of prices, the determinants of market value, and so forth. If engineering is about designing solutions to problems in a world of constraints and tradeoffs, which I think is a fair definition, the best engineering solutions can emerge only in the context of market prices and market forces. And engineers should take the lead in insisting that market forces be permitted to work as broadly as possible.

For example, pollution taxes and the trading of pollution credits are preferable to outright pollution controls or mandated solutions. The former allow an economic calculus of tradeoffs to enter the engineering model, and the later, not. To take another example, the Engineer of 2020 report cites the shortage of water as a pressing global need, and surely it is. But why? Because, universally, the price of water is regulated and held below a price that reflects its true value. The engineering solution ought to be to develop the right price and let market forces operate, not to waste precious resources solving a problem that fundamentally may not exist.

One of the best papers I read at Chicago suggested that we will never run out of any natural resource, as long as market forces are allowed to work. As relative scarcity raises the price, conservation, and more important, the development of new supplies and substitutes (which is what engineers are so darn good at doing) will take care of the problem. The point is that engineering and free-market economics necessarily advance hand-in-hand. The extreme case of communist countries, where market forces and the profit motive were closed off, proves the point. They resorted to stealing technology because they were unable to create it.

Unless the importance of free markets is understood, engineering can easily go the wrong way. The 2020 report quotes the Guiding Principles for Green Engineering, many of which read like Communist Party slogans. For example, Principle #6 is: "Strive to Prevent Waste." (I think I'll put that up on my living room wall in bright red letters.) But that statement is non-operative. The trouble is that striving itself is wasteful if the waste saved is not worthwhile. And how would one measure in the absence of a price for the waste? Again, engineers need market prices, not black-and-white regulations, to make correct, "unwasteful," economic decisions, and engineers should inject themselves forcefully into this very public debate.

While we're on the subject of waste, there is a form of waste in engineering that I think everyone will agree must be reduced. I was stunned to read that if all entering freshmen completed their engineering degrees, the number of graduates would increase by an astonishing 40 percent. To put that in the parlance of total quality management, the failure rate of American engineering departments is two out of five—hardly 6 sigma. If a for-profit company had a failure rate that high, it would go out of business. Something is terribly wrong here, and it must be fixed. Perhaps part of the fix is better preparation and better selection of students before they enter an engineering program.

Engineers have always yearned for more respect from, and authority in, society. They still clamor for it, I suspect. But if an answer has been to make engineers better engineers by making them more human, it is equally true that to make humans better humans they must become better engineers. (My sloganeering is definitely competing with Chairman Mao.) We must begin earlier imparting the mind-set of engineering to all students, not just engineering students, to help them understand the merits of using rational, economic models and discourse to solve problems, even before they enter college but also while they are in college. The challenge, I repeat, is not just to put the human in the engineer, but also to put the engineer in all humans. In this respect, engineering departments have failed miserably. They have not implanted the mind-set of the engineer in liberal arts students. Why is there a one-way street—we have to take their classes, and they make fun of us? We must reciprocate. Call it the revenge of the nerds.

In Bruce Seely's excellent review of engineering education reform, he closed with a passage from William Wickenden, a 1920s president of Case Institute of Technology. Wickenden wrote, "What appears to be the most needed is an enriched conception of engineering and its place in the social economy, a broader grounding in its principles and methods, and a more general postponement of specialized training to graduate schools"—and I paraphrase here—to entry-level jobs. Like Seely, I recommend this pithy summary, which seems to address some of the issues I have just raised.

As a closing note from the perspective of industry, let me say that in business we learn that whatever gets measured gets managed; the obverse is mostly true, too. My favorable impression of the work of the task force as represented in the Engineer of 2020 report was undermined by the paucity of specific, numerical goals. I urge you to quantify objectives, to set targets and milestones, and to develop a system of accountability and reward around achieving them. You must also be very careful to set goals for the right outcomes, because you might just get them in ways that make no sense. In fact, I wouldn't be above suggesting soliciting award funding from industry.

A related point is that engineering departments should not eschew industry relations but should embrace those connections, unabashedly and much more broadly and formally than they do today. Do not be concerned that you will be co-opted by mere commercial priorities, because they can never overcome the instinct for learning and discovery that is so strong in the engineering community. Look at funds as important market signals of how to allocate resources to problems that promise the biggest and most immediate "bang for the buck." I'd even like to get monetary incentives into faculty pay, but that is a topic for another day.

I know I've thrown out some tough challenges for you as tenured academics, but you owe it to yourselves and the future of engineering to rise to them. I earnestly thank you for hearing out this has-been engineer. And I close by imploring you to be generous when you grade my presentation. Thanks, again.

Educating Engineers for 2020 and Beyond

Charles M. Vest
Massachusetts Institute of Technology

I am very pleased to be playing a small role in these important deliberations about educating the engineer of 2020 and beyond. In his letter of invitation, Wayne Clough suggested that I explore this topic "particularly with respect to your extensive experience in higher education." That was probably his way of reminding me that I am approaching graybeard status. But it also gave me a chance to look back over my 35-plus years as an engineering educator. When I did, I realized that many things have changed remarkably, but others seem not to have changed at all.

The list of things that have not changed is long—far too long. Issues that are still with us, that have hardly changed during all these years, are: how to make the freshman year more exciting; how to explain what engineers actually do; how to improve the writing and communication skills of engineering graduates; how to bring the richness of American diversity into the engineering workforce; how to give students a basic understanding of business processes; and how to get students to think about professional ethics and social responsibility. But for the most part, change has been astounding. In the past 35 years, we have moved from slide rules to calculators to PCs to wireless laptops. Just think of all that implies.

Looking ahead to 2020, a mere 16 years in the future, and setting goals should be a "piece of cake." But is it? To gain some perspective, just look back 16 years and think about what was not going on in 1988.

There was no World Wide Web. Cell phones and wireless communication were in the embryonic stage. The big challenge was the inability of the American manufacturing sector to be competitive in world markets. Japan was about to bury us economically. The human genome had not been sequenced. There were no carbon nanotubes. Buckminster Fullerines had been around for about three years. We hadn't even started to inflate the dot-com bubble, let alone watch it burst. And terrorism was something that happened in other parts of the world—not on our shores.

All this is to say that predicting the future, or even setting meaningful goals, is a risky business . . . even on a scale of a mere 16 years. Years ago, I read that an author who made a study of predictions of the future found one simple invariant. We always underestimate the rate of technological change and overestimate the rate of social change. That is an important lesson for engineering educators because we educate and train the men and women who drive technological change. We turn them loose to affect, and work within, the developing social, economic, and political context.

Although Phase I of the Engineer of 2020 (creating the vision) has already been completed, I hope you will forgive me for making some observations about the context within which we must advance engineering education. These observations fall into five categories: (1) opportunities and challenges; (2) globalization; (3) scale and complexity; (4) new systems engineering; and (5) delivery and pedagogy.

OPPORTUNITY AND CHALLENGE

I envy the next generation of engineering students because this is the most exciting period in human history for science and engineering. Explosive advances in knowledge, instrumentation, communication, and computational capabilities have created mind-boggling possibilities for the next generation. The degree to which students are already routinely cutting across traditional disciplinary boundaries is unprecedented. Indeed, the distinction between science and engineering in some domains has been blurred to extinction, which raises some serious issues for engineering education.

As we think about the many challenges ahead, it is important to remember that students are driven by passion, curiosity, engagement, and dreams. Although we cannot know exactly what they should be taught, we must think about the environment in which they learn and the forces, ideas, inspiration, and empowering situations to which they are exposed. Despite our best efforts to plan their education, to a large extent we can simply wind them up and then step back and watch the amazing things they do. In the long run, making universities and engineering schools exciting, creative, adventurous, rigorous, demanding, and empowering milieus is more important than specifying curricular details.

GLOBALIZATION

Our task today is to focus on engineering education in the United States, but we can only do so in the context of engineering in 2020 and beyond. We have to ask basic questions about future engineers: who they will be; what they will do; where they will do it; why they will do it; and what this implies for engineering education in the United States and elsewhere.

The truth is that in the future American engineers will constitute a smaller and smaller fraction of the profession. More and more engineers will be educated and will work in other nations, especially in Asia and South Asia, and they will do just what our engineers do—work to run at the leading edge of innovation. Future engineers will be moving rapidly up the proverbial food chain. They will practice engineering in national settings and in global corporations, including corporations with headquarters in the United States. They will see engineering as an exciting career, a personal upward path, and a way to affect local economic well-being.

Universities around the world, especially in Asia and South Asia, are becoming increasingly utilitarian, focusing on advancing economies and cutting-edge research. Tectonic changes are taking place in the way engineers are being produced and in where engineering and research and development are being done.

From the U.S. perspective, globalization is not a choice; it is a reality. To compete in world markets in the "Knowledge Age," we cannot depend on geography, natural resources, cheap labor, or military might. We can only thrive on brainpower, organization, and innovation. Even agriculture, the one area in which the United States has traditionally been the low-cost producer, is undergoing a revolution that depends on information technology and biotechnology, that is, brainpower and innovation.

So, we must do two things: (1) discover new scientific knowledge and technological potential through research; and (2) drive high-end, sophisticated technology faster and better than anyone else. We must make the new discoveries, innovate continually, and drive the most sophisticated industries. We must also continue to get new products and services to market faster and better than anyone else. We must design, produce, and deliver to serve world markets. And we must recognize that there are natural global flows of industry and that the manufacturing of many goods will inevitably move from country to country according to their state of development. Manufacturing may start in the United States, then move to Taiwan, then to Korea, and then to China or India. These megashifts will occur faster and faster and will pose enormous challenges to our nation.

Meeting these challenges will require an accelerated commitment to engineering research and education. Research universities and their engineering schools will have to do many things simultaneously: advance the frontiers of fundamental science and technology; advance interdisciplinary work and learning; develop a new, broad approach to engineering systems; focus on technologies that address the most important problems facing the world; and recognize the global nature of all things technological.

SCALE AND COMPLEXITY

Now let's think a bit about engineering frontiers and the content of engineering education. There are two frontiers of engineering. Each of them has to do with scale, and each is associated with increasing complexity. One frontier has to do with smaller and smaller spatial scales and faster and faster time scales, the world of so-called bio/nano/info. This frontier has to do with the melding of the physical, life, and information sciences, and it has stunning new, unexplored possibilities. Natural forces of this world are forcing faculty and students to work together across traditional disciplinary boundaries. This frontier certainly meets the criterion of inspiring and exciting students. And out of this world will come new products and processes that will drive a new round of entrepreneurship . . . based on things you can drop on your toe and feel—real products that meet the real needs of real people.

The other frontier has to do with larger and larger systems of great complexity and, generally, of great importance to society. This is the world of energy, environment, food, manufacturing, product development, logistics, and communications. This frontier addresses some of the most daunting challenges to the future of the world. If we do our jobs right, these challenges will also resonate with our students.

NEW SYSTEMS ENGINEERING

I first heard the term "systems engineering" as a graduate student in a seminar about the Vanguard missile—the United States' first, ill-fated attempt to counter *Sputnik* by putting a grapefruit-sized satellite into space. An embarrassing number of Vanguards started to climb and then blew up. Khrushchev found this very funny. In fact, the Vanguard rocket was assembled from excellent components, but they had been designed with no knowledge of the components with which they would interface. As a result, heat, electrical fields, and so on, played havoc with them. The fix was to engineer the system. I found this very interesting . . . and then, like most students of that era, I pursued a career in engineering science.

But back to the present. Many of our colleagues believe that we must develop a new field of systems engineering and that it should play a central role in engineering education in the decades ahead. In 1998, MIT established an Engineering Systems Division, which reflected a growing awareness of the rising social and intellectual importance of complex engineered systems. At the time, a large number of faculty members in the School of Engineering and other schools at MIT were already engaged in research on engineering systems . . . and MIT had launched some very important educational initiatives at both the master's and doctoral levels.

The Engineering Systems Division is intended to provide a focus for these activities by giving them greater administrative and programmatic coherence and stimulating further development. MIT, of course, is famous for establishing "engineering science," which revolutionized engineering in the post-World War II era. In fact, in my view, the pivotal moment in MIT's history was when President Karl Compton realized that we could not be great in engineering if we did not also have great science. This realization started the institution on a path that led to the engineering science revolution.

Another pivotal moment in MIT's history occurred half a century ago when a faculty commission (headed by Warren K. Lewis) considering the nature of our educational programs told us that to be a great engineering school in the future we would have to develop strong programs in the humanities and social sciences. Perhaps that set us on a path to the evolving twenty-first-century view of engineering systems, which surely are not based solely on physics and chemistry. Indisputably, engineers of today and tomorrow must conceive and direct projects of enormous complexity that require a new, highly integrative view of engineering systems.

Academics led the way in engineering science, but I don't think we have led the way in what we now call "systems engineering." In fact, as we observe developments in industry, government, and society, we are asking ourselves what in the world we should teach our students. Although this is a valuable exercise, it is not enough. We need to establish a proper intellectual framework within which to study, understand, and develop large, complex engineered systems. As Bill Wulf [president of the National Academy of Engineering] has eloquently warned us, we work every day with systems whose complexity is so great that we cannot possibly know all of their possible end states. Under those circumstances, how can we ensure that they are safe, reliable, and resilient? In other words, how can we practice engineering?

Something exciting is happening, however, and it comes none too soon. The worlds of biology and neuroscience are suddenly rediscovering the full glory and immense complexity of even the simplest living systems. Engineers and computer scientists are suddenly as indispensable to research in the life sciences as the most brilliant reductionist biologists. The language is about circuits, networks, and pathways.

It is fascinating to participate in discussions of the role of science and biology—of research and development—in homeland security, or more generally in antiterrorism. I think of this as the "Mother of All Systems Problems." Designing systematic strategies to protect against terrorism has about as much in common with our experience of protecting ourselves from the Soviet threat of just a few years ago as it does with strategizing against eighteenth-century British troops marching toward us in orderly file.

Consider what IBM's vice president for research, Paul Horn, is thinking about these days. His company and his industry, which produce the ultimate fruit of the engineering science revolution (i.e., computers) is morphing into a new services sector—financial services, manufacturing services, McDonald's hamburger services. Paul Horn is asking himself if a services science is about to emerge. I don't know if a new discipline is about to appear, but if it does, it will be a subset of the new systems engineering.

I referred to homeland security as the Mother of All Systems Problems, but there is an even greater, and ultimately more important systems problem—that is the "sustainable development" of human societies on this system of ultimate complexity and fragility we call Earth. In Europe, sustainable development, ill defined though it may be, is part of the everyday work of industry and politicians and a common element in political rhetoric—and rhetoric is a start. I am troubled that sustainable development is not even on the radar screen in the United States, let alone on the tongues of presidential contenders. Nevertheless, sustainable development must be on our agenda as we prepare the engineers of 2020.

DELIVERY AND PEDAGOGY

So far, I have suggested that engineering students prepared for 2020 and beyond must be excited by their freshman year; must have an understanding of what engineers actually do; must write and communicate well; must appreciate and draw on the full richness of American diversity; must think clearly about ethics and social responsibility; must be adept at product development and high-quality manufacturing; must know how to merge the physical, life, and information sciences when working at the micro- and nanoscales; must know how to conceive, design, and operate engineering systems of great complexity. They must also work within a framework of sustainable development, be creative and innovative; understand business and organizations, and be prepared to live and work as global citizens. That is a tall order . . . perhaps even an impossible order.

But is it really? I meet kids in the hallways of MIT who can do all of these things—and more. So we must keep our sights high. But how are we going to accomplish all this teaching and learning? What has stayed constant, and what needs to be changed?

One constant is the need for a sound basis of science, engineering principles, and analytical capabilities. In my view, a strong base of fundamentals is still the most important thing we provide, because we really can't predict in detail what students will end up needing. And I am so old fashioned that I still believe great lectures are wonderful teaching and learning experiences. So humor me, and don't give up entirely on masterfully conceived, well delivered lectures. They still have their place . . . at least they better have, because at MIT we just built a magnificent, whacky, inspirational, and expensive building designed by Frank Gehry, and—by golly—it has classrooms and lecture halls in it (among other things). But even I admit that there is truth in what my extraordinary friend Murray Gel-Mann likes to say, "We need to move from the sage on the stage to the guide on the side." Studio teaching, team projects, open-ended problem solving, experiential learning, engagement in research, and the philosophy of CDIO (conceive/design/implement/operate) should be integral elements of engineering education.

Now for what has changed. Two obvious things have changed—we now have information technology, and we have the MTV generation. So the idea is to provide deep learning through instant gratification. It sounds oxymoronic to me . . . but it seems to be happening! Actually, our Frank Gehry building is about something like that.

Of course, I have to say something about the role of information technology in educating the engineer of 2020. But before I do, I want to tell you a true story. A few years ago, two dedicated MIT alums, Alex and Britt d'Arbeloff, gave us a very generous endowment, the d'Arbeloff Fund for Excellence in Education, which was inspired by Alex's desire to understand and capitalize on the role of information technology in teaching and learning on a residential campus. We celebrated the establishment of the fund with an intense, day-long, highly interactive forum on teaching that brought together a large number of our most innovative and talented teachers and a wide range of students.

At the end of that very exciting day, we all looked at each other and realized that nobody had actually talked about computers. Even though information technology is a powerful reality, an indispensable, rapidly developing, empowering tool, computers do not contain the essence of teaching and learning. These are deeply human activities. So we have to keep our means and ends straight.

In the first instance, the Internet, World Wide Web, and computers can do two things for engineering schools. First, they can send information outward, beyond the campus boundary. And second, they can bring the external world to the campus. By sending information out, we can teach, or better yet, provide teaching materials to teachers and learners all over the world. By bringing the world in, we can enrich learning, exploration, and discovery by our students.

Information technology can also create learning communities across time and distance. It can access, display, store, and manipulate unfathomable amounts of information, images, video, and sound. It can provide design tools and sophisticated simulations. And it can burn up a lot of money. To reduce the amount of money, we can do what the Internet and Web do best—create open environments and share resources and intellectual property across institutions. The goal of MIT's OpenCourseWare initiative is to make the basic teaching materials for 2,000 MIT courses available on the Web to teachers and learners anywhere, at any time, free of charge. For example, my remarkable colleague Jesus del Alamo is installing PCs in underresourced African universities, enabling students to log on and operate sophisticated and expensive experimental equipment that is physically located at MIT.

Information technology in education is important, but it is merely the paper and pencil of the twenty-first century. For engineering students of 2020, it should be like the air they breathe—simply there to be used, a means, not an end. But my secret desire, which I hope will play out on the time scale of the next 16 years or so, is that cognitive neuroscience will catch up with information technology and give us an understanding of the nature of experiential learning—a real science of learning. Then we might see a quantum leap, a true transformation in education.

IN THE MEANTIME . . .

In closing, I want to repeat something I said earlier. Making universities and engineering schools exciting, creative, adventurous, rigorous, demanding, and empowering milieus is more important than specifying curricular details. My primary advice for educating the engineer of 2020 is this. As you develop the concept of a new curriculum and new pedagogy, as you try to attract and interest students in nanoscale science, large complex systems, product development, sustainability, and business realities, don't be tempted to crowd the humanities, arts, and social sciences out of the curriculum. The integral role of these subjects in U.S. engineering education differentiates us from much of the rest of the world. I believe the humanities, arts, and social sciences are essential to the creative, explorative, open-minded environment and spirit necessary to educate the engineer of 2020.

American research universities, with their integration of learning, discovery, and doing, can still provide the best environment for educating engineers . . . if we support, sustain, and challenge them. We must retain their fundamental rigor and discipline, but also provide opportunities for as many undergraduates as possible to participate in research teams, perform challenging work in industry, and gain substantive professional experience in other countries.

One final, critical point—once we decide what to teach and how to teach it, we must be sure that the best and brightest young American men and women become our students . . . and the engineers of 2020 and beyond. In the past 16 years, the number of B.S. degrees in engineering granted in the United States dropped from about 85,000 to a low of 66,000; it has rebounded now to about 75,000. In this global, knowledge age with its serious problems and opportunities, we need the best and brightest students to pursue careers in engineering, and we need a large percentage of them to earn Ph.D.s in the areas of engineering that can lead to innovations that will keep us free, secure, healthy, and thriving in a vibrant economy.

This will require two things in addition to the broad objectives I have already discussed. First, we must double and redouble our efforts to make engineering schools and the engineering profession attractive and fully engaging to women and students in underinvolved minorities. We need equity and full participation in our engineering workforce, faculties, and leadership. Second, we should rally support for the growing movement to create a twenty-first-century analogue of the National Defense Education Act of the 1950s and 1960s.

I wish you all good luck with the tasks you have set for yourselves. And remember, we cannot afford to fail.

Appendix C

NAE Engineer of 2020
National Education Summit

National Academy of Engineering
2101 Constitution Ave. NW
Washington DC 20418

Thursday, July 22, 2004

8:00 a.m.   **Continental Breakfast—GREAT HALL**
8:45   **Opening and Welcome—AUDITORIUM**
         Wm. A. Wulf, President, National Academy of
         Engineering
         Stephen Director, Dean of Engineering, University
         of Michigan and Chair, NAE Committee on
         Engineering Education
         G. Wayne Clough, President, Georgia Institute of
         Technology and Chair, Engineer of 2020 Steering
         Committee

         SESSION I: CHAIR, G. Wayne Clough

9:10   **Keynote Presentation:**
         Engineering Education in the 21st Century: An
         Industry View
         Ruth David, President and CEO, ANSER

171

9:50   **Invited Panel: Innovation and Reform in Engineering Education**
   Panel Moderator, Ray Bowen, President Emeritus, Texas A&M University
   Gretchen Kalonji, Professor, University of Washington
   Arden Bement, Director, National Institute of Standards and Technology; Acting Director, National Science Foundation
   Linda Katehi, Dean, School of Engineering, Purdue University
   Bennett Stewart, III, Senior Partner, Stern Stewart & Co.
   Follow-on discussion and Q&A in Town Hall Meeting format

11:05   **BREAK—GREAT HALL**

11:30   **Keynote Presentation:**
   Engineering Education in the 21st Century: A University View
   Charles M. Vest, President, Massachusetts Institute of Technology

12:15 p.m.   **Lunch—THE REFECTORY**

   SESSION II: CHAIR, Wm. A. Wulf

12:45   **Address by Shirley Ann Jackson,** President, Rensselaer Polytechnic Institute

   SESSION III: CHAIR, G. Wayne Clough

1:15   **Review of Engineer of 2020 Phase I Report—AUDITORIUM**
   Alice Agogino, Professor, University of California, Berkeley
   Follow-on discussion and Q&A

1:45   **Statement of Charge to Breakout Teams**

2:00   **Breakout Sessions**

Attendees will be distributed among five breakout teams. The teams will be given the afternoon to respond to the team assignments. Teams can determine their own break schedules. Refreshments will be available throughout the afternoon.

A. An Education Philosophy and Strategy

Each breakout team is assigned an education philosophy below and is **charged to develop a strategy** for achieving the long-term goals of a successful engineering education model in 2020 within the framework represented by that philosophy.

Group 1, NAS 150
Leader, James Wagner, President, Emory University

Propose an undergraduate engineering education model(s) that meets the aspirations expressed in the Engineer of 2020 Report assuming conventional constraints are not binding. Consider how much of the conventional curriculum should be retained, e.g., the calculus requirement.

Group 2, NAS 180
Leader, David Daniel, Dean of Engineering, University of Illinois

Propose an undergraduate engineering education model(s) that comes as close as possible to meeting the aspirations expressed in the Engineer of 2020 Report while remaining within conventional constraints such as the "four-year" curriculum and ABET requirements. How will we add new knowledge in areas like nanotechnology?

Group 3, NAS 250
Leader, Stephen Director, Dean of
Engineering, University of Michigan

Propose new pedagogical approaches that
should be used to educate engineering
graduates for 2020 with respect to
accommodating differences in learning styles,
the changing nature of the student graduating
from high school, new options offered by
educational technology, problem-based
education, "just in time" material delivery, and
interdisciplinary education.

Group 4, Members Room
Leader, Alice Agogino, Professor, University of
California, Berkeley

Explore the role of undergraduate engineering
education in relation to liberal arts and social
studies, and public policy. What should
engineering do to promote preparation for
management, law, medicine, and other
professions? How should topics like
management and leadership be accommodated?

Group 5, NAS Board Room
Leader, Kent Fuchs, Dean of Engineering,
Cornell University

Propose revisions for department and faculty
roles needed to meet the engineering education
needs of graduates in the year 2020. Should all
engineering faculty be required to have a
Ph.D.? Should experience be required for
capstone courses? How can the professoriate be
diversified to better reflect the population at
large? Can department expectations allow for
flexibility in individual faculty expectations?

B. Setting an Action Agenda

Keeping in mind the philosophy assigned and strategy developed in part A, breakout teams will develop an action agenda to achieve their desired goals.

1. List the things in engineering education that should be changed immediately (short-term) and would not require significant support from external communities. Choose the three most important things on the list and describe the rationale for their selection.

2. List the things in engineering education that should be changed in the immediate or near-term but would likely require support from external communities. Choose the three most important things on the list and describe the rationale for their selection.

3. List the things in engineering education that should not be changed and that should be sustained in the new century. These will be considered constraints as the team develops plans to make the changes identified above.

4. Consider the questions listed in the addendum as the action agenda is being developed.

5:00   **Reception—GREAT HALL**

Friday, July 23, 2004

8:00 a.m.   **Continental Breakfast—GREAT HALL**

              SESSION IV: CHAIR, Wm. A. Wulf

9:00   **Review of Day 1—AUDITORIUM**
              G. Wayne Clough

9:30 **Keynote Address**
Engineering Education in the 21st Century:
An Industry View
Nicholas Donofrio, Senior Vice President,
Technology and Manufacturing, IBM

SESSION V: CHAIR, G. Wayne Clough

10:10 **Team Reports** with Q&A
Teams will present their proposed strategies and action
agendas to the full assembly. The audience will have an
opportunity to critique and react to the proposals.

11:25 **BREAK—Teams move to breakout rooms**
11:40 **Breakout Sessions—same meeting rooms**

Breakout teams meet to create action plans considering
feedback from the full assembly.

C.   Creating an Action Plan
   Prepare a plan to make the three most important
   immediate changes and the three most important
   near-term changes identified in step B above. Keep in
   mind the constraints the team has agreed upon in
   step B.3 above. The action plans should include
   short- and medium-term milestones as needed,
   metrics to assess and evaluate the impact of the
   recommended changes, and mechanisms for feedback
   and continuous improvement. Consider the
   questions below as the details of the plan are
   developed.

12:00 p.m. **Lunch** (working lunch served in breakout rooms)

1:30 **Plenary Session—AUDITORIUM**
Teams present their action plans.

2:45 **Closing Remarks** (Clough, Wulf)

3:00 **Adjourn**

ADDENDUM
POSSIBLE QUESTIONS FOR THE BREAKOUT SESSIONS

1. Outcome Goals for Engineering Graduates

a. What technical and professional knowledge should be expected of an individual called an "engineer" in 2020?

b. Given their likely social and political environments, what additional knowledge and skills will be required beyond those currently expected of engineering graduates (e.g., leadership, civic involvement, public policy, etc.)?

c. Will any skills currently assumed of engineering graduates be superfluous because of changes in technology or society?

d. What knowledge, skills, and abilities will best position domestic students to compete in a global marketplace?

e. How can formal education be better integrated with informal and lifelong learning by engineering graduates?

f. How do we attract and engage the broadest range of talent as future engineers?

g. How do we better provide fluency in operating in diverse intellectual and cultural environments to our graduates?

2. Curricula, Laboratories, and Learning Technologies

a. What experiences can we provide to best prepare our students for their future working environments?

b. How do we balance disciplinary depth with the interdisciplinary challenges of real-world problems?

c. How do we best address the technological knowledge needs of non-majors?

d. Should wider adoption be made of block scheduling and other efforts to overcome the tyranny of the current academic units such as the course and the semester?

3. Teaching, Learning, and Assessment Processes

a. How do we ensure the continuing currency of our curricula?

b. Can accreditation better recognize proficiency in teaching and learning practices or are alternative processes necessary?

c. How can assessments that better reflect the situations and knowledge that we will expect of graduates?

d. Out of class learning experiences can be valuable in broadening the education for an engineering graduate; how can we formalize activities like service, internships, leadership workshops, study abroad, team competitions, and so on?

4. Faculty, Departments, and Institutions

a. How do we better prepare current and future faculty for their roles as guides and mentors?

b. How can be better balance the teaching of practical and theoretical engineering knowledge and skills?

c. Can engineering departments accommodate a service course function as a means to address the needs of non-majors?

d. How do we overcome the barriers to departmental and institutional evolution and change?

e. Do we need to change and can we change the faculty reward and tenure systems?

5. External Influences and Constraints on Engineering Education

a. How can engineering education adapt to and engage an increasingly diverse student population?

b. How can engineering education better accommodate fluctuations in domestic and global economic cycles?

c. How can information technologies that allow the blurring of time and place best be exploited to provide flexible and continuing education?

d. How do we best anticipate and exploit consolidation within higher education?

e. What strategies will be necessary for the survival of engineering education in political environments where states (and corporations) invest less and less in higher education, but expect ever higher returns on their investments?

NAE ENGINEER OF 2020 NATIONAL EDUCATION SUMMIT

National Academy of Engineering
2101 Constitution Ave. NW
Washington DC 20418

Attendees

Alice Agogino*
President
Association of Academic Women,
    UC Berkeley
University of California, Berkeley
5136 Etcheverry Hall
Berkeley, CA 94720
P: 510-642-6450
aagogino@me.berkeley.edu

John Anderson
Provost and University Vice
    President
Case Western Reserve University
10900 Euclid Avenue
Cleveland, OH 44106-7001
P: 216-368-4346
johna@case.edu

Rich Anderson
President-elect
ABET
President, SOMAT
26445 Northline Road
Taylor, MI 48180
P: 734-946-1147

Tim Anderson
Professor
University of Florida
300 Weil Hall
Gainesville, FL 32611
P: 352-392-0946
tim@ufl.edu

Cynthia Atman
Director, Center for Engineering,
    Learning, and Teaching
University of Washington
Room 223, Engineering Annex
Box 352180
Seattle, WA 98195
P: 206-616-2171
atman@engr.washington.edu

Frank Barnes
Distinguished Professor
University of Colorado, Boulder
Engineering Center
ECOT 250
Boulder, CO 80309
P: 303-492-8225
barnes@colorado.edu

---

*Engineer of 2020 Phase II Committee Member.

Cathleen Barton
U.S. Education Manager
Intel
5000 W. Chandler Blvd.
CH2-135
Chandler, AZ 85226
P: 480-554-2514
cathleen.a.barton@intel.com

Arden Bement
Acting Director
National Science Foundation
4201 Wilson Blvd.
Arlington, VA 22230
P: 703-292-9232
abement@nsf.gov

Barry Benedict
Dean, College of Engineering
University of Texas at El Paso
Office of the Dean, E-230
500 West University Ave
El Paso, TX 79968
P: 915-747-5460
babenedict@utep.edu

Joe Bordogna
Deputy Director
National Science Foundation
4201 Wilson Boulevard
1205N
Arlington, VA 22230
P: 703-292-8001
jbordogn@nsf.gov

Anjan Bose
Dean, College of Engineering and
    Architecture
Washington State University
Dana 146
Pullman, WA 99164
P: 509-335-5593
bose@wsu.edu

Ray Bowen
President
Texas A&M University
MS 3123
Mechanical Engineering Dept.
College Station, TX 77843
P: 979-862-2955
r-bowen@tamu.edu

John Brighton
Assistant Director for Engineering
National Science Foundation
4201 Wilson Boulevard
505N
Arlington, VA 22230
P: 703-292-8300
jbrighto@nsf.gov

George Bugliarello
President Emeritus
Polytechnic University
6 Metrotech Center
Brooklyn, NY 11201
P: 718-260-3330
gbugliar@poly.edu

Ilene Busch-Vishniac
Professor
Johns Hopkins University
219 Latrobe Hall
Baltimore, MD 21218
P: 410-516-8777
ilenebv@jhu.edu

Slade Cargill
Chair, Department of Materials
    Science and Engineering
Lehigh University
Whitaker Laboratory
5 East Packer Avenue
Bethlehem, PA 18015
P: 610-758-4207
gsc3@lehigh.edu

RPH Chang
Director, Materials Research
    Institute
Northwestern University
2220 Campus Drive
Evanston, IL 60208
P: 847-491-3537
r-chang@northwestern.edu

Paul Citron
Retired VP, Technology Policy and
    Academic Relations
Medtronic
710 Medtronic Parkway, NE
Minneapolis, MN 55432
P: 763-505-2924
paulcitron@msn.com

Wayne Clough*
(Chair, steering committee)
President
Georgia Institute of Technology
225 North Avenue, NW
Atlanta, GA 30332
P: 404-894-5051
wayne.clough@carnegie.gatech.edu

David Craig
Director, Application Development
Reliant Energy
1201 Louisiana Street, #884
Houston, TX 77022
P: 713-488-4321
ggray01@reliant.com

David Daniel
Dean, College of Engineering
University of Illinois, Urbana-
    Champaign
306 Engineering Hall, MC 266
1308 W. Green Street
Urbana, IL 61801
P: 217-333-2150
dedaniel@uiuc.edu

Ruth David
President and CEO
ANSER
2900 S. Quincy Street
Suite 800
Arlington, VA 22206
P: 703-416-3197
ruth.david@anser.org

Lance Davis
Executive Officer
National Academy of Engineering
500 Fifth Street, NW
Washington, DC 20001
P: 202-334-3677
ldavis@nae.edu

Eugene Deloatch
Dean, College of Engineering
Morgan State University
Room 118, Engineering Building
Baltimore, MD 21251
P: 443-885-3231
deloatch@eng.morgan.edu

Warren DeVries
Division Director, ENG/DMII
National Science Foundation
4201 Wilson Blvd.
Arlington, VA 22230
P: 703-292-8330
wdevries@nsf.gov

Rick Dill
Hitachi Global Storage
650 Harry Road, C1
San Jose, CA 95120
P: 408-323-7228
rick.dill@hgst.com

Stephen W. Director
Robert J. Vlasic Dean of
    Engineering
University of Michigan
1221 Beal Avenue
Ann Arbor, MI 48109-2102
P: 734-647-7010
director@umich.edu

Nick Donofrio
Senior Vice President
IBM
New Orchard Road
Armonk, NY 10504
P: 914-499-4200
nmd@us.ibm.com

Dianne Dorland
Dean, College of Engineering
Rowan University
Rowan Hall
Glassboro, NJ 08028
P: 856.256.5300
dorland@rowan.edu

James Duderstadt
President Emeritus
University of Michigan
2001 Media Union
Ann Arbor, MI 48109
P: 734-647-7300
jjd@umich.edu

Glen Ellis
Professor of Engineering Education
Smith College
Pickering Engineering Program
Northampton, MA 01063
P: 413-585-4598
gellis@email.smith.edu

Don Falkenburg
Director, Greenfield Coalition for
    New Manufacturing
    Education
Wayne State University
87 E. Ferry Rd.
Detroit, MI 48202
P: 313-874-7010
falken@mie.eng.wayne.edu

Pat Farrell
Director of CAE
College of Engineering
University of Wisconsin-Madison
2630 Engineering Hall
1415 Engineering Drive
Madison, WI 53706
P: 608-262-3484
farrell@engr.wisc.edu

Norman Fortenberry
Director, Center for the
    Advancement of Scholarship
    on Engineering Education
National Academy of Engineering
500 Fifth Street, NW
Washington, DC 20001
P: 202-334-1926
nfortenb@nae.edu

Eli Fromm
Professor
Drexel University
CAT 179
Philadelphia, PA 19104
P: 215-895-2201
fromme@drexel.edu

Jeff Froyd
Foundation Coalition
Texas A&M
3578 TAMU
College Station, TX 77843
P: 979-845-7574
froyd@tamu.edu

Kent Fuchs
Dean, College of Engineering
Cornell University
Carpenter Hall
Ithaca, NY 14853-2201
P: 607-255-9679
engineering_dean@cornell.edu

Don Giddens
Dean, College of Engineering
Georgia Tech
225 North Avenue
Atlanta, GA 30332-0360
P: 404-894-6825
don.giddens@coe.gatech.edu

Deborah Grubbe*
Corporate Director, Safety and
    Health
DuPont Company
1007 Market St.
D. 6064
Wilmington, DE 19898
P: 302-773-0299
deborah.l.grubbe@usa.dupont.com

Esin Gulari
Division Director, ENG/CTS
National Science Foundation
4201 Wilson Blvd.
Arlington, VA 22230
P: 703-292-8370
egulari@nsf.gov

Bruce Hamilton
Division Director, ENG/BES
National Science Foundation
4201 Wilson Blvd.
Arlington, VA 22230
P: 703-292-8320
bhamilto@nsf.gov

Jeanette Harrison
Director, Knowledge & Learning
Intel Corporation
5000 West Chandler Blvd.
MS CH2-152
Chandler, AZ 85226
P: 480-554-2277
jeanette.k.harrison@intel.com

Randy Hinrichs*
Group Program Manager
Learning Science and Technology
Microsoft Corporation
1 Microsoft Way
Redmond, WA 98052
P: 425-703-5524
randyh@microsoft.com

Frank Huband
Executive Director
ASEE
1818 N Street, NW
Suite 600
Washington, DC 20036
P: 202-331-3545
f.huband@asee.org

Shirley Ann Jackson
President
RPI
President's Office
110 8th Street
Troy Building
Troy, NY 12180
P: 518-276-6211
president@rpi.edu

Leah Jamieson
Associate Dean of Engineering
Purdue University
465 Northwestern Avenue
West Lafayette, IN 47907
P: 765-494-4966
lhj@purdue.edu

Jim Johnson
Dean, College of Engineering
Howard University
Downing Hall
Washington, DC 20059
P: 202-806-6577
jj@scs.howard.edu

Kristina Johnson
Dean, College of Engineering
Duke University
305 Teer Building
Box 90271
Durham, NC 27708
P: 919-660-5386
tammy.sorrell@duke.edu

Wayne Johnson
Executive Director, Worldwide
    University Relations
Hewlett-Packard Corp.
1501 Page Mill Rd
MS 1167
Palo Alto, CA 94304
P: 650-857-4257
wayne.johnson@hp.com

Marshall Jones
Sr. Mechanical Engineer
GE Corporate R&D
One Research Circle
Building KW, Room C289
Niskayuna, NY 12309
P: 518-387-5528
jonesmg@crd.ge.com

Russel Jones
President, WFEO Committee on
    Capacity Building
2001 Mayfair McLean Court
Falls Church, VA 22043
RCJonesPE@aol.com

Gretchen Kalonji
Kyocera Professor of Materials
    Science
University of Washington
302 Roberts Hall
Box 352120
Seattle, WA 98195
P: 206-543-1151
kalonji@u.washington.edu

Linda Katehi
Dean of Engineering
Purdue University
400 Centennial Mall Drive
West Lafayette, IN 47907
P: 765-494-5346
katehi@ecn.purdue.edu

Alan Kay
Senior Fellow
Hewlett-Packard
1209 Grand Central Avenue
Glendale, CA 91201
P: 818-332-3003
alan.kay@hp.com

Sue Kemnitzer
Dep. Division Director
National Science Foundation
Division of Engineering Education
    and Centers
4201 Wilson Blvd.
585N
Arlington, VA 22230
P: 703-292-8383
skemnitz@nsf.gov

Bruce Kramer
Director, Division of Engineering
     Education and Centers
National Science Foundation
4201 Wilson Blvd.
585N
Arlington, VA 22230
P: 703-292-8380
bkramer@nsf.gov

John Linehan
Vice President
Whitaker Foundation
1700 N. Moore Street
Arlington, VA 22209
P: 703-528-2430
linehan@whitaker.org

Tom Mahoney
Principal, QB Analysis
4023 Greystone Drive
Morgantown, WV 26508
P: 304-594-0319
tcmahoney@mindspring.com

Louis Martin-Vega
Dean, College of Engineering
University of South Florida
ENB135
Tampa, FL 33620
P: 813-974-3780
lmartinv@eng.usf.edu

Mary Mattis
Staff Officer
National Academy of Engineering
500 Fifth Street, NW
Washington, DC 20001
P: 202-334-2041
mmattis@nae.edu

Gary May
Professor, School of Electrical and
     Computer Engineering
Georgia Tech
Van Leer Electrical Engineering
     Bldg.
777 Atlantic Drive, NW
Atlanta, GA 30332
P: 404-894-9420
gary.may@ece.gatech.edu

Lueny Morell
Hewlett Packard
University Relations, HP Labs
1501 Page Mill Road
Palo Alto, CA 94304
P: 787-819-7418
lueny.morell@hp.com

Alfred Moye*
Former Director of University
     Relations
Hewlett-Packard
124 Gramercy Drive
San Mateo, CA 94402
P: 650-347-1132
alfred.moye@hp.com

Carol Muller
President and CEO
MentorNet
San Jose State University
One Washington Square
San Jose, CA 95192
P: 408-924-4065
cbmuller@mentornet.net

John Mulvey
Founding Member, Bendheim
    Center for Finance
Princeton University
26 Prospect Avenue
Princeton, NJ 08540
P: 609-258-5423
mulvey@princeton.edu

Vijaya Narapareddy
Associate Professor, School of
    Management
University of Denver
2199 S. University Blvd.
BA 438, DCB
Denver, CO 80208
P: 303-871-2198
vnarapar@du.edu

Priscilla Nelson
Senior Advisor, ENG/OAD
National Science Foundation
4201 Wilson Blvd.
Arlington, VA 22230
P: 703-292-7018
pnelson@nsf.gov

Mal O'Neill
CTO
Lockheed Martin Corp
6801 Rockledge Drive
Mail Point 380
Bethesda, MD 20817
P: 301-897-6867
mal.o'neill@lmco.com

Simon Ostrach*
Wilbert J. Austin Distinguished
    Professor of Engineering
Case Western Reserve University
103 Crawford Hall
10900 Euclid Avenue
Cleveland, OH 44106
P: 216-368-0749
sostrach@ncmr.org

Jamie Ostroha
National Materials Advisory Board
National Research Council
500 Fifth Street, NW
Washington, DC 20001
P: 202-334-3505
jostroha@nas.edu

Panos Papamichalis
Chairman, Department of
    Electrical Engineering
Southern Methodist University
3145 Dyer Street
Dallas, TX 75275
P: 214-768-4905
panos@engr.smu.edu

Ron Paulson
Vice President
Lockheed Martin Corporation
Engineering and Engineering
    Process Improvement
6801 Rockledge Drive
Mail Point 380
Bethesda, MD 20817

Paul Peercy
Dean, College of Engineering
University of Wisconsin-Madison
1415 Engineering Drive
Madison, WI 53706
P: 608-262-3482
peercy@engr.wisc.edu

Catherine Peters
Associate Dean for Academic
    Affairs, School of Engineering
    and Applied Science
Princeton University
C-222, Engineering Quad
Princeton, NJ 08544
P: 609-258-5645
cap@princeton.edu

George Peterson
President
ABET
111 Market Place
Suite 1050
Baltimore, MD 21202
P: 410-347-7700

Russ Pimmel
Lead Program Director, Division of
    Undergraduate Education
National Science Foundation
4201 Wilson Blvd.
Arlington, VA 22230
P: 703-292-4618
rpimmel@nsf.gov

James Plummer
Dean of Engineering
Stanford University
Terman Engineering Center,
    Room 214
Stanford, CA 94305
P: 650-723-3938
plummer@ee.stanford.edu

Lynn Preston
Deputy Division Director, ENG/
    EEC
National Science Foundation
4201 Wilson Blvd.
Arlington, VA 22230
P: 703-292-8381
lpreston@nsf.gov

Michael Reischmann
Deputy Assistant Director, ENG/
    OAD
National Science Foundation
4201 Wilson Blvd.
Arlington, VA 22230
P: 703-292-8301
mreischm@nsf.gov

Mike Roco
Senior Advisor for Nanotechnology
National Science Foundation
4201 Wilson Blvd.
Arlington, VA 22230
P: 703-292-8301
mroco@nsf.gov

Jeff Russell
Chair, Civil Engineering
University of Wisconsin-Madison
2258 Engineering Hall
1415 Engineering Drive
Madison, WI 53706
P: 608-262-7244
russell@engr.wisc.edu

James Schaffer
Professor and Director of
    Engineering
Lafayette College
308 Acopian Engineering Center
Easton, PA 18042
P: 610-330-5403
schaffej@lafayette.edu

Lyle Schwartz
Director
Air Force Office of Scientific
    Research
4015 Wilson Blvd. #713
Arlington, VA 22203
P: 703-696-7551
lyle.schwartz@afosr.af.mil

Elane Scott
Future Workforce Strategist
    Consultant
The Boeing Company
11044 Thesis Avenue
Whittier, CA 90604
P: 562-797-4358
elane.v.scott@boeing.com

Bruce Seely
Chair, Department of Social
    Sciences
Michigan Technological University
1400 Townsend Drive
Houghton, MI 49931
P: 906-487-2113
bseely@mtu.edu

Subrata Sengupta
Dean, College of Engineering
University of Michigan-Dearborn
2180 Engineering Complex
Dearborn, MI 48128
P: 313-593-5290
razal@engin.umd.umich.edu

Ernest Smerdon*
Emeritus Dean of Engineering
University of Arizona
Tucson, AZ 85721
P: 520-577-7464
ej6721@aol.com

Lee Snapp
Dean, College of Engineering
Salish Kootenai College
Indigenous Math and Science
    Institute
PO Box 70
Pablo, MT 59855
P: 406-275-4800
lee_snapp@skc.edu

Bennett Stewart
Senior Partner
Stern Stewart and Company
135 East 57th, 22nd Floor
New York, NY 10022
P: 212-261-0747
gbstewart@sternstewart.com

William Sullivan
Senior Scholar, Co-director of the
    Preparation for the
    Professions Program
Carnegie Foundation for the
    Advancement of Teaching
51 Vista Lane
Stanford, CA 94305-8703
P: 650-566-5100
Sullivan@carnegiefoundation.org

Richard Taber
Corporate and Foundations
    Relations Consultant
National Science Foundation
4201 Wilson Blvd.
Arlington, VA 22230
P: 703-292-4639
rtaber@nsf.gov

Galip Ulsoy
Director, ENG/CMS
National Science Foundation
4201 Wilson Blvd.
Arlington, VA 22230
P: 703-292-8360
aulsoy@nsf.gov

Usha Varshney
Program Director, ENG/ECS
National Science Foundation
4201 Wilson Blvd.
Arlington, VA 22230
P: 703-292-8339
uvarshne@nsf.gov

Charles Vest
President
MIT
77 Massachusetts Ave., Rm 3-208
Cambridge, MA 02139-4307
P: 617-253-0044
cmvest@mit.edu

James Wagner
President
Emory University
201 Dowman Drive
408 Administration Bldg.
Atlanta, GA 30322
P: 404-727-6013
wagner@emory.edu

Ardie Walser
Associate Dean, Engineering
    Administration
City College of New York
138th Street and Convent Avenue
New York, NY 10031
P: 212-650-7000
walser@ccny.cuny.edu

Bevlee Watford
Associate Dean for Academic
   Affairs
Virginia Tech
212 Hancock Hall (0275)
Blacksburg, VA 24061
P: 540-231-3244
deuce@vt.edu

Karan Watson*
Associate Provost and Dean of
   Faculties
Texas A&M University
607 Rudder Tower
1126 TAMU
College Station, TX 77843
P: 979-845-4274
watson@tamu.edu

Barbara Waugh
Co-founder, Worldwide
   e-Inclusion
Hewlett-Packard Labs
1501 Page Mill Road,
   MS 1167
Palo Alto, CA 94304
P: 650-857-2273
barbara.waugh@hp.com

James Williams
Dean, College of Engineering
Ohio State
142 Hitchcock Hall
2070 Neil Avenue
Columbus, OH 43210
P: 614-292-2651
williams.1726@osu.edu

David Wisler*
Manager, University Programs and
   Aero Technology Labs
GE Aircraft Engines
M/S A411
1 Neumann Way
Cincinnati, OH 45215
P: 513-243-2905
dave.wisler@ae.ge.com

David Wormley
Dean of Engineering
Pennsylvania State University
101 Hammond Bldg.
University Park, PA 16802
P: 814-865-7537
dnwdo@engr.psu.edu

Wm. A. Wulf
President
National Academy of Engineering
2101 Constitution Ave., NW
Washington, DC 20001
P: 202-334-3201
wwulf@nae.edu